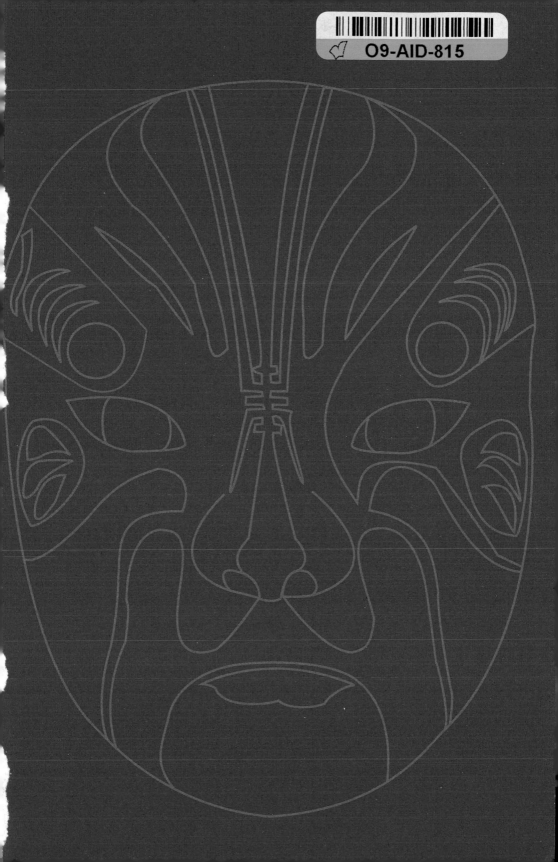

China's Creative Imperative

How Creativity is Transforming
Society and Business in China

China's Creative Imperative

How Creativity is Transforming Society and Business in China

Kunal Sinha

WILEY

John Wiley & Sons (Asia) Pte. Ltd.

This publication is designed to provide accurate and authoritative information in regard to the subject matter covered. It is sold with the understanding that the publisher is not engaged in rendering professional services. If professional advice or other expert assistance is required, the services of a competent professional person should be sought.

Other Wiley Editorial Offices

John Wiley & Sons, Inc., 111 River Street, Hoboken, NJ 07030, USA
John Wiley & Sons Ltd., The Atrium Southern Gate, Chichester PO19 8SQ, England
John Wiley & Sons (Canada) Ltd., 5353 Dundas Street West, Suite 400, Toronto,
       Ontario, M9B 6HB, Canada
John Wiley & Sons Australia, Ltd., 42 McDougall Street, Milton, Queensland 4064,
       Australia
Wiley-VCH, Boschstrasse 12, D-69469 Weinheim, Germany

Library of Congress Cataloging-in-Publication Data
978-0-470-823859

Typeset in 11 points, ITC Galliard by Hot Fusion
Printed in Singapore by Saik Wah Press Ltd.
10 9 8 7 6 5 4 3 2 1

This book is dedicated to the memory of my father,
Late Professor Madan Mohan Sinha

CONTENTS

Foreword

Everywhere I have gone for the past decade—to CEO gatherings, industry events, and client meetings—I have been asked what Ogilvy knows about China. As head of the largest Western marketing communications company in that country, and one with Chinese leadership at the unit's helm, I thought this a fair request. It is easy for me to talk about our own operations and our clients' interests in this booming economy. But there is need for a broader perspective.

It is easy to see that China is emerging from decades of cultural and economic repression. It is obvious that the country is moving from rigid communism to controlled capitalism, and is joining the world economy in a weighty position. What this means for us in the West is access to a great volume of inexpensive labor, broad and deep manufacturing capability, and new markets for our own goods.

But there is so much more to understand about China. It is not just the volume of workers or the size of markets to consider. There are thousands of years of history. The more we know about China's cultural past, its historic sweep of intellectual curiosity and invention, the better we will be able to understand this giant of the 21st century. And the more we see how these historical and cultural implications live on in the China of today, the better able we will be to deal with this remarkable country.

This is why this book was written. Our team in China, led by Kunal Sinha, undertook the ambitious job of researching and writing a survey of Chinese creativity down through time and then across the contemporary landscape. It depicts a distinctive creative spirit that is informed by history and is forming China's future. It is one part history book, one part contemporary cultural observation, and one part a prescriptive approach to China as a business partner. Above all, this book looks at how creative thinking, rooted in a long history, is different in China—where it is more collective than individual, more proactive than reactive, more realistic than abstract.

Creativity is in ascendancy everywhere in the world. We would be wise to understand the Chinese perspective. This book, I hope, will help erase preconceived notions of what should be in "the China Discussion," and will help us all better understand and embrace the people of China.

Shelly Lazarus
Chairman and CEO
Ogilvy & Mather Worldwide
January 9, 2008

Why creativity matters in China

These days, it's almost marketing orthodoxy to compare China to a slumbering dragon. Invariably, the dragon is described as slowly awakening, the metaphor being that when the creature comes fully awake, the rest of the world had better watch out. Imagine the disposable income of over a billion people!

But what no one ever really asks is this: Is China, the dragon, waking up as a happy camper (say, like Snow White) or as a cranky old lady with an axe to grind (say, like her jealous stepmother)? And like Rip Van Winkle, is China ready for what the world has become in the time it's been sleeping?

The other orthodoxy making the rounds is whether Beijing and Shanghai have it in themselves to be creative forces that can be ranked alongside the likes of New York, Tokyo, or Paris. Sure it built the Great Wall, but that was a few years ago. Does it have any juice left to punch in its own weight category? And isn't this the country that's better known for its counterfeit handbags?

Harsh judgments. And more than a little unfair.

People always forget that it's only been in the past couple of decades—a blink of an eye in its 5,000-year history—that China has had the time and energy to think about something beyond its own political, cultural, and social needs. In terms of Maslow's hierarchy of needs, China has, until recently, been preoccupied with producing basic necessities such as food and manufactured goods. Who has time to reinvent the toilet brush (like Philippe Starck did) when there are railway tracks to be laid, iron smelters to be built, and 1.3 billion people to feed, educate and house? In other words, all the dull, quotidian necessities of survival.

The fact is, the Chinese haven't been having an easy time over the past 100 years. Barely a century ago, it began the first in a series of seismic revolutions, beginning with the toppling of the Qing dynasty in 1911, followed by the long years of internal discord, an ugly and painful war with Japan, then a civil war between Chiang Kai-shek's Nationalists and Mao Zedong's Communists. And in the aftermath of Mao's victory in 1949, the glow was quickly replaced by one calamitous social policy after other, among them the disastrous Great Leap Forward and the unimaginable Cultural Revolution.

So, the question "Does creativity matter in China?" (or even, "Does China have what it takes?") brings its own peculiar riposte: "Yes, of course we do, but please stop harping about it. We're a little busy right now."

But if ever a country had a theme song, China's would be Gloria Gaynor's "I Will Survive."

Like the over-extended housewife at the end of a very long day, China is only now (re)discovering its awesome talent for creativity —or what Mark Earls in his wonderfully lucid book *Welcome to the Creative Age*, has called "the vision of novel contents."

The signs all point to a renaissance by a country that's ready to bring about its own vision of novel contents and participate fully in the global creative economy. For a country whose name in Chinese means "Middle Kingdom"—the center of the world— the stakes are high: nothing less than the reclamation of its rightful place under the sun. Why else do Beijing, Shanghai, Nanjing, Guangzhou, and a thousand other Chinese cities shake, day and night, to the drones, pounding, and whirs of countless piling drills, hammers, and cranes? (Here, I'm reminded of Mao's aphorism that in order to create, we have to destroy.) Why else are the local newspapers filled with ads offering English lessons and deportment classes on how to dress to impress, or even how to use Western-style cutlery?

The cinema and art world—always reliable barometers of a country's mood—are bubbling away: postmodernists such as Zheng Fan Zhi and Zhou Chunya beguile, while Chen Kaige and Zhang Yimou continue to examine China's vast repertoire of social issues and aspirations.

What the world is only just starting to cotton on to is that the slumbering dragon woke up some time ago. It's sitting up, yawning, and rubbing its eyes. And it's hungry. Starving, in fact. It's been a long hibernation and China is ready to hit the road running. And like Snow White's wicked stepmother, it's a little cranky that it's got so much lost ground to make up.

It's got critical mass on its side, too. On some level, everyone knows this, of course, but they've never really understood how huge China is, both literally and metaphorically. For instance, there are more than 1,000 advertising agencies in Shanghai alone. Greater China has 350 million middle income households—that's the equivalent of the United States, Europe, the Middle East, and Africa combined.

And if you ever needed a barometer of China's naked ambition, look no further than the 2008 summer Olympic Games. Ancient Beijing has been transformed (though not always in a good way) into a metropolis of antique palaces and juiced up architectural hubris by the likes of Herzog and de Meuron, Andreu, and Koolhaas. The Commune by the Great Wall, a complex of experimental buildings that's been transformed into sprawling hotel suites, is booked solid, while the former American legation is now a hive of buzzy art galleries and restaurants. Old quarters are being repackaged as creative hubs for artists, musicians, filmmakers, and designers. Even the air is being vacuumed clean.

So, yes, creativity matters in China. It matters a lot; for the Chinese realize that the country that gave the world gunpowder, silk, navigational tools, and fireworks still has the chops to deliver. And then some. But that's never been the issue. When you've had the creative genius to plan and build the only man-made structure that's visible from space (well, almost), you get a kind of inbuilt confidence that there's not a lot you can't do.

And, more importantly, you never really lose that confidence.

We've always known that China was a creative force to be reckoned with. The real question is how, in this brave new world that it's woken up in, China can be more than a producer of cheap toys and fake Louis Vuitton bags.

For those of us in the marketing and advertising field, that's the fun question to try and answer. Watching it all unfold. And if we're brave enough, hitching our wagon to this playful dragon and hanging on for the ride of our lives.

Free of the pretense of "everyone is born equal," China is finally at a stage where it doesn't always have to play catch up to everyone else. May the best man win. If China has anything to say about things, that man is going to be Chinese.

And if you were to look at China's track record to date, I wouldn't bet on the other guy. As Kunal Sinha makes clear in the following pages, neither would he.

Tham Khai Meng
Co–chairman, Ogilvy & Mather Asia Pacific

Acknowledgments

This book is the result of a year-long journey through China's creative landscape, and I have had many guides along the journey. The idea of the project was born at a meeting held in Beijing in November 2005. T.B. Song, chairman of Ogilvy & Mather Greater China, Joseph Wang, vice chairman, and Shenan Chuang, CEO, felt the need for this endeavor and were wonderful supporters of the venture. The book would not have been possible, however, without the splendid efforts of my team members Jane Ling and Kate Gong. (Jane and Kate also took the photographs on pages 97 and 155, and 161, respectively.) For over a year, they interpreted Chinese culture for me, as well as conducted and translated most of the interviews and discussions with the creative people and "people on the street" who are profiled in its pages. In addition, they dug into the literature to find further evidence of the resurgence of creativity in China. Even when I fell ill for more than six months, they kept the momentum going. Carly Lee and Sarah Xu in Beijing pitched in as well. Edward Bell was a very helpful sounding board in the initial stages, suggesting perspectives and questions that we could explore. Paul Matheson was helpful in reframing the questions. Kweichee Lam at Ogilvy Beijing and C.J. Hwu, publishing editor at John Wiley, reviewed the manuscript and suggested valuable changes. Robyn Flemming was a fantastic editor; weeding out the unnecessary, helping clarify context and content, and pushing for accuracy. Janis Soo coodinated the production of the book superbly. And they both did all that with remarkable speed. Thank you ever so much for adding so much to the manuscript, Robyn and Janis.

I owe immense gratitude to all the people we interviewed; they are all busy folks, but they found the time to speak with us and walk us through their business enterprises. Zhang Fan, Zhou Yi, Tim Richter, Victoria Lu, Fang Fang, Su Yong, Lin Di, Li Jia, Chen Yuanyuan, Shen Lihui, Joecy Wu, Zhang Haisheng, Wei Wei, Huang Yi Xin, Zhang Yuan, Liu Miao Miao, Liu Fendou, Yao Yingjia, Jenny Ji, Zhang Bolin, and He Yan: thank you very much for your stories and your insights. May your ventures prosper and may your creative flame burn forever.

My wife Sumona and our little daughter Sukanya kept my spirits up and nursed me back to health, both physically and mentally. Sumona was an eager listener during the time I spent researching and writing the book, as I shared with her stories of my encounters with some very interesting people. Above all, I thank God for looking after me in my tough times.

Genesis

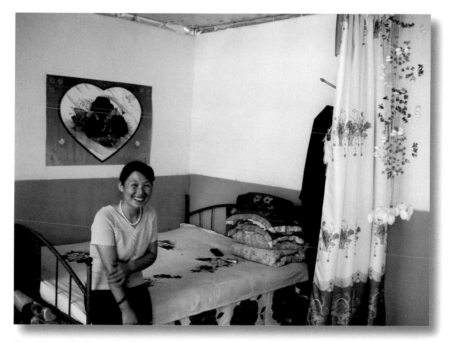

Mrs. Yang in her Linxia home

It happened during my first visit to China. I was wandering along neon-lit Wangfujing Pedestrian Street in Beijing with three colleagues, when two young Chinese girls approached us and struck up a conversation. They spoke reasonably good English, enquired where we were from and how long we would be in Beijing, and then popped the question: "Would you like to buy some paintings? We are art students and are holding an exhibition nearby." We looked at each other, wondering if it was a setup, but finding comfort in our number.

As we four Indian men, aged in our thirties, were led by the girls along a narrow lane, up a flight of stairs, and into a door-lined corridor, our sense of anticipation was palpable. One of the girls knocked softly on a door, and it opened up; inside, from floor to ceiling, were displayed paintings: landscapes in watercolors, street scenes, depictions of the human form, and abstracts in oils, inspired by China past and present. The girls and their friends from art school were indeed selling their work.

We were entirely unsure about the prices they quoted and left empty-handed, to the disappointment of the students. Two days later, in the fashionable 798 Art District in Dashanzi, we attended a wine-tasting session in an art gallery where paintings of a similar nature hung on the walls, with price tags upward of US$2,000.

This was my first taste of China's appetite for creativity. I discovered later that there are something like 68 million committed art collectors in China.[1] Between them, China's 4,000 auction houses sold US$1.3 billion worth of art in 2005.[2]

Eight months later, my team member Jane Ling and I were in the home of a family of relatively modest means in the small town of Linxia in Gansu province. Yang Dezhi worked odd jobs, usually as an electrician and mechanic. A sewing machine stood in one corner of the room. His wife said she stitched clothes for a tailor in the neighborhood. In spite of their apparently hard times, their home was neat, with little touches of beauty—such as a poster with a big floral heart that decorated one wall.

Atop the TV set rested a beautiful swan made of paper. We asked Mrs. Yang if she had made it. "Oh, yes," she said, almost apologetically. "I make these. My friends say it is quite uniquely designed. I sell them for 20–40 yuan [approximately US$3–5], depending on the size. All my neighbors, friends, and relatives know I make them, and they tell others. That's how I get my customers." Mrs. Yang's skills and ideas may not have been on the same scale as the artists in Beijing's 798 Art District, but her creativity had earned her both popularity and profit.

In May 2006, Technorati, the world's leading weblog search engine, proclaimed that the most popular blog in the world, with more than 50 million hits, was written by Xu Jinglei. If you don't live in China or cyberspace, chances are you would be saying, *Xu who?*

Model—actress–singer—filmmaker—blogger—webpreneur, that's who. Xu Jinglei epitomizes the modern-day Chinese creative artist, one whose abilities and interests transcend any one medium. Born in Beijing, Xu Jinglei enrolled in the prestigious Beijing Film Academy in 1993. She was soon appearing as a supporting actress in movies and TV dramas such as *Xing Yan Qing Shi Dai* (*New Love Era*, 1994), *Yi Chang Feng Hua Xue Yue De Shi* (*A Romantic Love Story*, 1995), and *Beijing Love Story* (1996). After graduating from the academy in 1997, Xu Jinglei continued to appear in TV series and films, achieving moderate popularity and winning the Chinese Film Society Performance Award for her first major film role in Zhang Yang's *Spicy Love Soup* (1997), the Golden Rooster Award for Best Supporting Actress in *Far from Home* (*Yu Zhong*, 2002), and the Baihua Best Actress Award for *I Love You* (*Zhang Yuan*, 2003). Her first feature film as director, *Wo He Ba Ba* (*My Father and I*, 2003), was rewarded at home with a Golden Rooster for Best Directing Debut and was invited to a number of international film festivals. This success served as a springboard for her second feature, *Letter from an Unknown Woman* (2004), an imaginative and mature adaptation of Stefan Zweig's 1922 novella of the same name (previously filmed by Max Ophüls in 1948). Xu Jinglei's film won the Silver Seashell Award at the San Sebastian Film Festival in Spain in 2004.

Even as she continued to act and direct, Jinglei began writing her blog in October 2005. What does she write about? Daily stuff such as her pet cat, her friend's wedding, her work schedule, and, in mid-2007, her experiences during a six-week language course she attended in New York. Sometimes she just writes about her thoughts and opinions on life. In an unobtrusive sort of way, she promotes her work through her writing.

In June 2006, by now a cyberspace veteran, she launched her first music album, *Dream Sheds Light on Reality*, through producer Taihe Rye's Digital Music distribution platform for the Internet and mobile phones. Then, drawing on calligraphy skills taught her by her father, she spent two months handwriting more than 6,700 Chinese characters to create a new font. The Founder Group, China's second-largest personal computer vendor, digitized the font, developed a software package to install it—and promptly put it on sale on Xu Jinglei's website for approximately US$1.35. By the time hackers broke into the site the next day and made the font available for free, she had already made quite a sum.

Art student, small-town resident, thirty-something celebrity, all united by a common urge to use their creative abilities to find a place in China's dynamic society. To me, they are symbolic of the sentiment that seems to be engulfing China: *We are not content with being the world's factory; we want to be the world's studio, too.* At another level, they represent a much larger population—those who have traditionally been bludgeoned into thinking, dressing, and speaking alike and have been thought incapable of making leaps of imagination. The overwhelming popularity of Xu Jinglei's blog, and the tiny market for Mrs. Yang's paper swans, both point to the fact that people in contemporary China are seeking out and valuing creativity in a way never before seen in that country—or, indeed, anywhere else in the world. When one has to compete with more than a billion people to make oneself heard and recognized, the only way of doing it is by being creative.

In mid-2006, we at Ogilvy & Mather China embarked on an ambitious journey in an attempt to understand how Chinese society and business are being transformed by this creative urge. It is, as we have concluded, a creative imperative. Whether it is a student attempting to be noticed by a recruiting company, or a small clothes store—one among scores of businesses—in the underground "Fashion Lady" market in Nanjing, or a poor migrant laborer with only 25 square feet of space to live in, or a Vienna-bound music composer—all have creative potential that is demanding to be unleashed. What you will read about in the pages of this book will undoubtedly make you rethink China's potential.

But before we examine the reasons and inspiration for its current creative resurgence, we must first go back in time, nearly 4,000 years, to gain a true appreciation of China's cultural roots.

---

[1]   People's Daily Online, May 14, 2006:
      http://english.people.com.cn/200605/14/eng20060514_265549.html.

[2]   Allen T. Cheng, "Art Rush Gains Steam in China," *Bloomberg News*, July 18, 2006.

A Short Cultural History of China

The glorious, inventive tradition

"Great indeed is the sublimity of the Creative, to which all beings owe their beginning and which permeates all heaven."

I Ching

The Chinese people have shared a cultural history that predates any other group in the world. When they settled in the Hwang Ho (Yellow River) valley in around 3000 BC, they were already farming, and using pottery, wheels, and silk. Archeological excavations have unearthed two kinds of pottery—red clay pots with black designs from Yangshao village in Henan province, and smooth black pottery from Lungshan in Shandong province, in northeast China. The period between 2070 and 1600 BC is referred to as the "Golden Age of Bronze." Two achievements stand out among the accomplishments of this period in China: the development of writing, and the discovery and production on a massive scale of bronze for weapons and ritual vessels used by the ruling class.

The Chinese form of writing—a complex system of picture writing, using pictograms, ideograms, and phonograms—developed during the Shang dynasty (c. 1766–1122 BC). The writings came to be known through the excavation of oracle bones, which were animal bones—mainly ox scapulae—and tortoise shells with writings inscribed on them. These were used in ancient China for keeping records and fortune-telling. The rulers of the Shang dynasty were very superstitious and so divination was a daily activity for almost everything, from weather and farming, to health and fortune. The divination questions or topics were often directed at ancestors, whom the ancient Chinese revered and worshipped, as well as at natural powers and Di, the highest god in Shang society.

The earliest bronze vessels were excavated from Erlitou, near the middle reaches of the Yellow River. Archeologists identify this site with the Xia dynasty (c. 2100–1600 BC), the earliest of the Three Dynasties—Xia, Shang, and Zhou—mentioned in ancient texts. Bronze casting attained its pinnacle during the Shang dynasty, whose kings ruled over much of northern China from their capitals at Zhengzhou and Anyang on the Yellow River. In 1976, archeologists at Anyang discovered the intact grave of Fu Hao, a consort of the Shang king. Fu Hao was buried in around 1200 BC in a tomb of moderate size that also contained 16 human skeletons (probably sacrificial victims), ivory goblets, 700 pieces of jade, and more than 200 ritual bronze vessels. This gravesite exemplified the skill of Shang bronze casters in transforming functional objects into works of sculpture. Most of the bronzes would have been used in life, but some were probably made specifically for the grave. Inscriptions on the sides of the vessels reveal that their function was to serve as ritual offerings of food and wine to ancestral spirits.

Given the abundance of liquor goblets dating back to the Shang dynasty, it seems that the Shang rulers were indulgent in their use of alcohol. The last of the Three Dynasties, the Zhou, overthrew the Shang royal house in around 1050 BC, justifying their conquest by citing the drunken excesses of the Shang kings. As evidence of their reaction to such excess, the bronze vessels found in Zhou tombs were used for preparing or serving food, rather than for wine.

Ox-shaped zun (wine vessel), Late Spring and Autumn period

Overlapping these two developments during this phase of Chinese history was the development of the *I Ching* (*The Book of Changes*). The oldest of the Chinese classic texts, it lays down a system of symbols designed to identify order in what seem like chance events, and describes an ancient system of cosmology and philosophy that is at the heart of Chinese cultural beliefs. The book consists of the symbols, rules for manipulating them, poems, and commentary. Traditionally, it was believed that the principles of the *I Ching* originated with the mythical Fu Xi, one of the earliest legendary rulers of China (traditional dates 2852–2738 BC).[1]

Of especial interest in the *I Ching* is its references to creativity. When it postulates that "Creativity comes from awakening and directing men's higher natures, which originate in the primal depths of the universe and are appointed by Heaven," it is saying that creativity is indeed a higher-order quality, which might be the preserve of a few who are "awakened." It also suggests that one of the qualities that a creative being possesses is that of recognition of an original idea. "The Creative knows the great beginnings. The Receptive completes the finished things." But then it goes on to suggest a role for creativity in times of adversity: "A person in danger should not try to escape at one stroke. He should first calmly hold his own, then be satisfied with small gains, which will come by creative adaptations." The *I Ching* contains the seeds and the inspiration for creativity in contemporary China, as we shall see later in this book.

It was between 770 and 476 BC, during the Chunqiu and Zhanguo era, that Chinese philosophy took root. The philosophy of Confucius, who lived during this time (c. 551–479 BC), emphasized personal and governmental morality, correctness of social relationships, justice, and sincerity. In his teachings, which his disciples organized and turned into *The Analects*, he presented himself as a "transmitter who invented nothing."[2] It is perhaps this credo, as much as his disciples' interpretations of his teachings into a very elaborate system of rules and practices, that gave birth to the didactic nature of Confucius's beliefs. Confucius is often considered a great proponent of conservatism, but a closer look at what he proposed often shows that he used—and possibly twisted—past institutions and rites to push a new political agenda of his own: rulers (not lords of states) to be chosen on merit, not parentage— rulers who were devoted to their people, and rulers who reached for perfection. Later rulers found it convenient to remind the Chinese population about Confucius every time they desired order and discipline in society. Confucianism also emphasized harmony with other people, not difference. *Rén* is the virtue of perfectly fulfilling one's responsibilities toward others, often translated as "benevolence" or "humaneness."

Chinese literature finds its origin with *Shijing* (*The Book of Odes*), an anthology of poems and hymns composed between the Zhou dynasty (1027–771 BC) and the Spring and Autumn Period (770–476 BC). Geographically, the works can be traced, once again, to the Yellow River basin. It was said that the 305 poems in *Shijing* could all be sung as songs. According to the tunes they were sung by, the poems were divided into three categories: *Feng* (Ballads), *Ya* (Festal Odes), and *Song* (Sacrificial Songs). Most of the poems in *Feng* are folk songs from along the Yellow River. Only a few of them were works of the nobles. *Ya* consists of 105 poems written by the nobles. *Song* consists of 40 poems, including the sacrificial hymns and songs in the courts of *Zhou*, *Lu*, and *Shang*.

In general, the poems from the common people are rich in

content, fresh in style, and varied in form, while those written by the nobles lack the flavor of poetry and seem inferior.[3]

Written on bamboo strips, and consisting of 58 chapters, the *Shang Shu* (*Book of History*) is a collection of the historical literature of ancient China. It records the sayings of the governors in the Shang and Zhou dynasties. The first five chapters purport to preserve the sayings and recall the deeds of such illustrious emperors as Yao and Shun, who reigned during the legendary age; the next four are devoted to the Xia dynasty, the historicity of which hasn't been definitively established; and the next 17 chapters deal with the Shang dynasty and its collapse. The blame for this is placed on the last Shang ruler, who is described as oppressive, murderous, extravagant, and lustful. The final 32 chapters cover the Zhou dynasty until the reign of Duke Mu of Qin. The book survived the book-burning movement and the war between Chu and Han, thanks to Fu Sheng, the court academician of the Qin dynasty (221–206 BC), who hid it inside the palace walls.

Qin Shi Huangdi founded the Qin dynasty in 247 BC and was the first emperor of a unified China from 221 BC until his death in 210 BC. Work on his grand mausoleum had begun in 246 BC. Some 700,000 workers and craftsmen toiled for 38 years to finish the empire that Shi Huangdi would rule in his afterlife. It would serve as a demonstration of the power, grandness, and prosperity of Qin Shi Huangdi's kingdom.

Qin Shi Huangdi's necropolis complex was constructed to serve as an imperial palace. It comprises several offices, halls, and other structures, and is surrounded by a wall with gateway entrances. The first emperor was buried alongside great amounts of treasure and objects of craftsmanship, as well as a scale replica of the universe complete with gemmed ceilings representing the cosmos, and flowing mercury representing the great earthly bodies of water. Pearls were also placed on the ceilings in the tomb to represent the stars and planets. But the most dramatic part of the tomb was the Terracotta Army—a collection of 8,099 life-sized, lifelike soldiers and horses that formed part of his troops—whose purpose was to protect the emperor. The soldiers, none of whom look alike, vary in height, uniform, and hairstyle in accordance with their military rank. The colored lacquer finish, molded faces, and real weapons and armor used in manufacturing these figures give them a realistic appearance. Over the centuries, the Terracotta Army has survived looting—when most of the weapons were removed—and a fire that burned for three months and destroyed the wooden superstructure. In its own inimitable way, the Terracotta Army is symbolic of the resilience of Chinese culture amidst war and invasion.

The Han dynasty (206 BC – AD 219), which followed the Qin dynasty, was a phase in Chinese history characterized by several important inventions and significant creativity. Many of the scientific discoveries made during this era would not be known to the Western world until many centuries later.

Pottery figures playing the bamboo flute and lute, Eastern-Han dynasty

In 120 BC, Han Wu Di set up YueFu, a government department where music staff were trained and folk songs collected. YueFu was not a Han dynasty invention, but Han Wu Di expanded it greatly. His aim was to revolutionize traditional rural temple music. YueFu prospered until 70 BC, when it was terminated due to financial constraints. YueFu is still recognized for its role during the early Han era, and the term is used to describe later Chinese poems written in a folk-song style.

Paper was invented by the Chinese in around 200 BC, and the paper-makers quickly mastered the techniques of bleaching and ungluing. But most of the paper at the time was made out of hemp. Almost 200 years later, Marquis Cai Lun of the Eastern Han dynasty used inexpensive materials such as tree, hemp ends, tattered cloth, and broken fishing nets to make paper. This paper was used daily and was popularly known as Cai Lun paper. Even though he didn't invent paper-making, Cai drew upon his predecessors' experiences and improved the technology for making paper. Cai Lun paper was light and thin, strong and inexpensive, and could be mass-produced. From then on, paper began to replace bamboo or wooden strips and silk for writing. Cai's contribution is considered to be one of the most important inventions in history, since it enabled China to develop and record its civilization much faster than with earlier writing materials.

Scale model of Zhang Heng's seismograph

In AD 132, the Han dynasty scientist Zhang Heng invented the first seismograph, used to detect the location of earthquakes. In AD 138, the seismograph detected an earthquake in Long Xi, at a distance of some 700 kilometers. According to the *History of the Later Han Dynasty* (AD 25–220), Zhang Heng's seismograph was an urn-like instrument with a central pendulum. An earth tremor would unbalance the pendulum, which would activate a set of levers inside. One of the eight replica dragons placed around the outside of the urn would then release from its mouth a bronze ball, which would fall into the mouth of a toad below. In this way, the timing and direction of an earthquake could be determined.

Sundials and water clocks were also invented during this time, when the day was divided into 12 periods and the lunar calendar devised. The Chinese were the first to use the place value system, whereby the value of a component of a number is indicated by its placement. Other practical inventions were those of the wheelbarrow, locks, and waterwheels to control the movement of water in streams and canals.

It was during the reign of Emperor Han Wu Di that the most authoritative work on Chinese history was written. Sima Tan was the prefect of the grand scribes in the imperial court. His son, Sima Qian, who succeeded him in that position, studied under the famous Confucian scholars of the age—Kong Anguo and Dong Zhongshu—as well as under his father, and became well versed in the history of the previous eras. When he was aged 20, he started to travel throughout the country, collecting useful first-hand historical records for his main work, *Shiji*. Although the style and form of Chinese historical writings have varied through the ages, Sima Qian's *Shiji* has dictated their quality. Interestingly, despite his official position as prefect of the grand scribes, Sima Qian refused to write *Shiji* as an official historiography. *Shiji* recorded the activities not only of those of high rank, but also of people of the lower class, so as to portray the darker side of the dynasty; thus, *Shiji* is regarded as a veritable record of the times.

With *Shiji*, Sima Qian initiated a new writing style by presenting history in the form of a series of biographies. Its artistry was reflected mainly in the skillful portrayal of many distinctive characters, based on true historical information. Sima Qian was also adept at illustrating the responses of the characters by placing them in sharp confrontation and letting their words and deeds speak for them. His inclusion of conversations also made the descriptions vibrant and realistic. The language was informal and humorous. His style was concise, but included comments on the historical events he was recounting. He avoided giving general descriptions. Instead, he tried to catch the essence of the events, and to portray the characters concretely and vividly. The resulting work had strong artistic appeal. The skilled use of characterization and plotting would also influence fiction writing, especially the classical short stories of the middle and late medieval Tang and Ming periods.[4]

Buddhism was introduced to China at the end of the Eastern Han dynasty, in the early third century. According to historical records, Emperor Ming Di of the Eastern Han dynasty dreamed of a golden man flying above his courtyard. The emperor sent two noblemen, Cai Yin and Qin Jing, as envoys from Luoyang, in Henan province, to China's western regions to learn about Buddhism and to invite the Buddha to return with them. The two envoys underwent much hardship on their journey, during which they met two eminent Indian monks, She Moteng and Zhu Falan. Cai Yin and Qin Jing returned to Luoyang with the monks, accompanied by a white horse carrying the sutras, or Buddhist scriptures. Emperor Ming Di ordered the construction of a temple to the north of the imperial road outside the city's Xiyong gate. The White Horse Temple, built in the style of Indian temples and named for the horse that had carried the sutras, was where She Moteng and Zhu Falan translated the sutras and wrote sermons.

Although the Chinese had used characters to write as early as 4,600 years ago, in the time of the legendary Yellow Emperor, and though the oracle bones and pottery mentioned earlier bore calligraphic inscriptions, these were not considered to be part of a mature language. Chinese calligraphy first bloomed as an art form in the Han dynasty. Many gifted calligraphers appeared around this time, usually producing their works anonymously. As they reached a very high level of art, the works produced in the Han dynasty became the prototype and set high standards for later calligraphers such as Wang Hsi-Chih and those of the Tang dynasty.

Most calligraphy styles were formed and reached their maturity during the Han dynasty. When the Western Han dynasty was established, Prime Minister Xiao He, an officer of the late Chin dynasty, was put in charge of making the ordinances and laws. The law required eight scripts "*Ba Ti*" to be the scripts of examinations. Good calligraphy in the examinations would fetch the writer a good government position. The most useful script in

Ba Ti was Li Shu, which was highly regarded because of its simplicity, structure, beauty, elegance, and design.[5] Thus, Li Shu became the most important script to study. Throughout the 400 years of the Han dynasty, almost all tablets were written in Li Shu.

The political instability that followed the Han period resulted in a greatly diminished cultural output. China remained divided for three-and-a-half centuries, with three kingdoms dominating: the Wei in the north, Shu Han in the southwest, and Wu in the southeast.

The only form of creativity that emerged during this period was the construction of Buddhist

Cowrie container with eight yaks, Western Han dynasty

grottoes under the patronage of the Wei. The construction of Yungang Grotto began in 460. It was constructed to please the emperor, Wen Cheng Di, and to refute the notion that there was no Buddha. The second phase of grotto excavation was done during the reign of his successor, Emperor Xiao Wen Di, from 470 to 494. From then on, the power of China's emperors was closely related to Buddhism. Commoners, officials, and monks could all provide funds to build the grotto, so that Yungang became an important religious site for Buddhists. The art style of Yungang Grotto came from three sources: the original tradition of Chinese statues, the influence of primarily Buddhist Sri Lanka, and the influence of Islamic Pakistan and Afghanistan.

The construction of the Longmen Grottoes began in 493, also during the reign of Emperor Xiao Wen Di, and continued through the succeeding six dynasties, including the Tang and the Song, that spanned over 400 years. Altogether, there are 1,352 caves, 785 niches, more than 97,000 statues of the Buddha, Bodhisattvas, and Arhats, and 3,680 inscribed stone tablets along the one-kilometer-long cliff of Mt. Longmen on the western, and Mt. Xiangshan on the eastern, sides of the Yihe River, south of Luoyang. According to UNESCO, the sculptures of the Longmen Grottoes are an outstanding manifestation of human artistic creativity. One-third of these cave sculptures date back to the Northern Wei dynasty, and two-thirds to the Tang dynasty. The style of sculpture, the design of the clothing, and the facial expressions on the statues, as well as the carving methods, show little foreign influence. These works represent the pinnacle of the development of Chinese grotto art.

The reunification of southern and northern China was marked by the Sui dynasty, founded by Emperor Wen (also known as Yang Jian), which had its capital at Chang'an (a suburb of present-day Xi'an). Although the Sui was a relatively short Chinese dynasty, it marked the construction of the Grand Canal, which linked the Huang, Huai, and Yangtze rivers, and saw various reforms by Emperor Wen and by Yangdi, his successor: the land equalization system was initiated to reduce the social divide between rich and poor, which resulted in enhanced agricultural productivity; governmental power was centralized; and coinage was standardized and unified. But the tyrannical demands of the empire, in the form of high taxes and compulsory labor, led to its rapid downfall. In a coup, army leader Li Shih-min defeated the imperial army, installed his father as emperor, and subsequently took over the throne as Emperor T'ai Tsung, in 626. It was the beginning of the Tang dynasty.

Historians regard the Tang dynasty, with its capital at Chang'an, the most populous city in the world at the time, as a high point in Chinese civilization equal, or even superior, to the Han period. Its territory, acquired through the military exploits of its early rulers, was greater than that of the Han. Stimulated by contact with India and the Middle East, the empire saw a flowering of creativity in many fields.

In Chinese history and folklore, Wu Daoxi is referred to as the "Painting God." Born in Yangzhai (Yu county in Henan province), Wu lost both his parents at a young age and lived a hard life in his early years. He learned from folk artists and sculptors how to make a living. Because Wu studied hard and was talented, by the time he was 20 years of age he had earned himself a good reputation as a painter. Emperor Xuanzong invited Wu to be an imperial painter in the court, giving him the name "Daoxuan." As an imperial painter, Wu painted only at the emperor's request, which he may have found very restrictive. On the other hand, the court provided the best living conditions and was an outlet for other forms of artistic creativity. Wu's character was unrestrained, direct, and indifferent to trivial matters, and it is known that he always drank while painting. It is also said that when Wu drew the halo around Buddha's head in a mural, he used his brushes without drafting the measurements first. Whenever he painted at Longxing Temple, it was always packed with observers. Wu moved his brush quickly, and most of his works were accomplished in a single session. Chang'an was the cultural center of its time, home to many famous men of letters and artists. Wu had many opportunities to stay with them, which helped improve his painting skills.

Wu mostly created religious murals, but his abundant works had a wide range of subjects. According to records, Wu painted over 300 murals and more than 100 scrolls. While many of them took as their subject Buddhism and Taoism, Wu also drew mountains, rivers, flowers, and birds. *The Presentation of Buddha* is his most representative work. Unlike his predecessor Gu Kaizhi, whose line strokes were slender and forceful but lacked variety, Wu's strokes were full of change and vigor, expressing the internal world of his subjects. Wu was always in great ferment when he was painting, and his works are an exhibition of his expressive style.

The Tang period was also the golden age of literature. A government system supported by a large class of Confucian literati selected through civil service examinations was perfected under the Tang rulers. This competitive procedure was designed to draw the best talent into government. But perhaps an even greater consideration for the Tang rulers, aware that imperial dependence on powerful aristocratic families and warlords would have destabilizing consequences, was to create a body of career officials having no autonomous territorial or functional power base. As it turned out, these scholar-officials acquired status in their local communities, family ties, and shared values that connected them to the imperial court. From Tang times until the closing days of the Qing dynasty in 1911, scholar-officials functioned often as intermediaries between the grass-roots level and the government.

The passion for literature saw its greatest manifestation in poetry. Beginning with the founder of the dynasty, down to the last ruler, almost every one of the emperors was a great lover and patron of poetry, and many were poets themselves. Through the influence of the Empress Wu Chao, or the "Woman Emperor" (684–704), poetry became a required subject in examinations for degrees and an important course leading to official promotion. This made every official, as well as every scholar, a poet. There were around 2,200 Tang poets whose works, totaling more than 48,900 pieces, have been preserved. The period between 700 and 780 is regarded as the most celebrated epoch of poetry. Its representative figures are Li Po (705–762), the genie of poetry; Du Fu (712–770), the sage of poetry; Wang Wei (699–759) and Meng Hano-jan (680–740), the two hermit-poets; and Ts'en Ts'an (awarded degree, 744) and Wei Ying-wu (740–830), the two magistrate-poets.

Li Po, a leader of the romantic school, rebelled against poetic conventions, as he did against society in general. Passionate and un-ruly, he embraced the realm of the immortals, whence, he claimed, he had been exiled to this world. Li Po was at his best when he sang of love and friendship; of the delights of wine; and of the strange, majestic, and awe-inspiring aspects of nature.

> Among the blossoms, a single jar of wine.
> No one here, I ladle it out myself.
> Raising my cup, I toast the bright moon,
> and facing my shadow makes friends three,
> Though the moon has never understood wine,
> and shadow only trails along behind me.
> Kindred a moment with moon and shadow,
> I've found a joy that must infuse spring:
> I sing, and moon rocks back and forth;
> I dance, and shadow tumbles into pieces.
> Sober, we're together and happy. Drunk,
> we scatter away into our own directions:
> intimates forever, we'll wander carefree
> and meet again in Star River distances.[6]

Generally considered to be China's greatest poet, Du Fu was a keen observer of the political and social scene who criticized injustice wherever he found it and clearly understood the nature of the great upheaval following the rebellion of dissatisfied generals in 755, which was a turning point in the fortunes of the Tang. As an artist, Du Fu excelled in all verse forms, transcending all rules and regulations in prosody while conforming to and exploiting them. His power and passion can perhaps be suggested by a single line:

Blue is the smoke of war, white the bones of men.[7]

Wang Wei, a meditative philosopher and painter with Buddhist inclinations, depicted the serenity of nature's beauty; it has been said that poetry is in his pictures and pictures are in his poems.

The Tang dynasty was known for a type of glazed pottery with the dominant colors of yellow, brown, and green. Unlike the more practical pottery of the earlier era, these were often used as burial objects. The pottery was mostly produced in Xi'an, Luoyang, and Yangzhou, all important cities along the Silk Road. The figures were a mix of accurately proportioned humans and animals with fluid lines, natural expressions, and life-like movements. The soldier figures had strong muscles and staring eyes, and wielded swords and arrows. The female figures had high hair buns, wore full-sleeved dresses, and stood gracefully erect. The animal figures, mainly horses and camels, had resolute expressions representing the hardships associated with traveling on the long road.

The opening up of the Silk Road during the Tang dynasty saw an influx of new cultural influences into China. The Silk Road was not only the channel for transporting merchandise, but also the medium by which forms, styles, fashions, and music were exchanged between the East and West. For instance, Persian music was appreciated in the palace of the Tang emperor; Persian food was served at the tables of the gentry; and women's clothing styles were inspired by Persia, India, and the central Asian nations. Orchestras played music derived from the kingdoms of Central Asia, with their distinctive instruments such as flutes, percussion (gongs and drums), stringed instruments, harps, lutes, and the pipa of Iran. At the same time, the Japanese kimono was influenced by colors worn by women of the elite class of the Tang dynasty, as was the styling of traditional Korean clothing.

The strong economy and powerful military force during the Tang era created a stable and prosperous society that provided a favorable environment for artists to create new works. At the same time, the influence of other cultures, thanks to an open-door policy enabled by trade, provided a stimulus for creators and propelled the Tang dynasty to its eminent status in China's creative history. Do you notice shades of contemporary China?

The Song dynasty (960–1279) was a culturally rich period in China for the arts, philosophy, and social life; a time of cultural consolidation. The era is often called the "Chinese Renaissance," because—similar to the European Renaissance—progress in the areas of technology and inventions, and new philosophical interpretations of the old texts, led to a renewal of the old as well as the creation of new streams. Landscape art and portrait painting were brought to new levels of maturity and complexity, and social elites gathered to view and to trade in precious artworks. During the Song period, even regular people enjoyed a vibrant social and domestic life. There were entertainment quarters in the cities, such as in Hangzhou, with a constant array of puppeteers, acrobats, storytellers, singers, and prostitutes; as well as places to relax, such as tea houses, restaurants, and organized banquets.

Shan shui, or landscape painting, first rose to wide prominence during the Song era. The name literally translates to *mountain-water-picture*. It was characterized by a group of landscape painters, most of them already famous—such as Xu Xi, Zhao Gan, Wang Qihan, Zhou Wenju, and Wei Xian—who produced large-scale landscape paintings. The paintings usually took mountains as their subject. Mountains had long been seen as sacred places in China; being close to the heavens, they were viewed as being the homes of the immortals. Some commentators have suggested that the Taoist emphasis on how minor the human presence is in the vastness of the cosmos, or the Neo-Confucian interest in the patterns or principles that underlie all phenomena, natural and social, explain the highly structuralized nature of *shan shui* painting. When Chinese artists paint a *shan shui* painting, they attempt to present not an image of what they have seen in nature, but what they have thought about nature. They are not concerned with whether or not the painted colors and shapes look like the real object.

Three important inventions of mankind date from the Song period: movable-type printing, gunpowder, and the compass. Two factors contributed to the technological leap that occurred during this historical period. The first was China's economic development, with the increasing importance of money as currency. The second factor was the organized civil bureaucracy of the Chinese state, which actively sought to enhance productivity in every sector of state life.

The invention of movable-type printing (*huozi yinshua*) by Bi Sheng greatly contributed to the spread of literature, knowledge, and thought. Song-era movable type was initially made from clay, and later from wood. The cheaper it became to produce books, the more widespread was literature of all kinds; on this basis, the first private libraries were acquired by the gentry. One of the first books printed using movable type was the Buddhist canon *Dazangjing* of 983. Many other books of literary or scientific content printed during the Song period have been preserved until today. Paper money and bills of exchange (*jiaozi*) were likewise produced using the new printing methods invented during the Northern Song period.

A very important innovation in war technology was the invention of gunpowder (*huoyao*) during the Tang period, which found applications only from the time of the Song dynasty. During the 11th century, firearms were already widespread among the Song, Khitan, and Jurchen troops. These arms were catapults (*paoshiji*) that launched bombs (*huoyaobao*) and grenades (*jili huoqiu*), some filled with poisonous evaporating materials. From the beginning of the 12th century, cannons (*pao*) were produced with barrels made from bamboo strips held together with iron rings.[8]

The Song dynasty was notable for the development of cities, not only for administrative purposes but also as centers of trade, industry, and maritime commerce. Private trade grew, and a market economy began to link the coastal provinces and the interior.

The Neo-Confucian philosopher Zhu Xi (1130–1200) synthesized Confucian thought and Buddhist, Taoist, and other ideas that became the official imperial ideology from late Song times to the late 19th century. Once incorporated into the examination system, Zhu Xi's philosophy evolved into a rigid official creed, which stressed the one-sided obligations of obedience and compliance of subject to ruler, child to father, wife to husband, and younger brother to elder brother. The effect was to inhibit the societal development of pre-modern China, resulting both in many generations of political, social, and spiritual stability and in a slowness of cultural and institutional change up to the 19th century. While it began with a renaissance, Song culture was also a culmination of the heritage of 2,000 years of culture. From this point of crystallization onward, Chinese thinking became orthodox, and culture became sterile as if it had been unchanged for thousands of years.

In the 13th century, it took the marauding Mongols 40 years to conquer China. The slowness of the conquest was due partially to topographical hindrances such as the mountains, but also the Chinese already had long experience with intruding nomadic tribes and had developed almost perfect defense instruments.

The Mongols set up the Yuan dynasty, which lasted for about 160 years (1206–1368). The founder of the dynasty was the brilliant general and statesman, Kublai Khan. His major achievement was to reconcile China to the idea of rule by a foreign people who had hitherto proven themselves to be great warriors but poor at governance. The effects of the Mongol rule can be observed in two fields. Because Chinese intellectuals were prohibited from achieving high positions within the bureaucracy, they withdrew and engaged in arts and literature. Novels, vernacular literature, and popular theater became acceptable literary genres for the higher educated. Songs sung in the taverns and marketplaces, and popular theater plays, were written down. The typical song and poem of the Yuan dynasty is the *qu*, or aria, which was also part of operas or theater plays. The second effect of Mongol rule was seen in the authoritarian style of government of the subsequent Ming dynasty.

The political interruption of Mongol rule didn't have an intensive impact on the arts in China. Superficially, the Mongol ruling elite adopted Chinese customs and habits. The development of the porcelain production technique went on, but the motifs changed. During the Yuan dynasty, the typical blue-white chinaware with a dragon motif became popular. Painters liked to depict scenes of the ruling elite engaging in activities such as horse racing. One of the more significant events during the Yuan dynasty was the Venetian Marco Polo's visit to the Yuan capital, Khanbalik (Dadu), now Beijing. Kublai Khan was so impressed by the visitor, he instructed his officials to accompany him on his tours across China. Marco Polo lived in China for 17 years, and his accounts of Chinese civilization stunned Europe upon his return.

In May 2007, Christie's of London sold at auction in Hong Kong a rare underglazed copper-red Ming dynasty (1368–1644) vase for US$10.13 million, setting a world auction record for a Chinese work of art. Even then, the Ming era in Chinese history was a time characterized more by displays of power, than by creativity.

The founder of the Ming dynasty, Zhu Yuanzhang, was a poor man when he joined the Red Turban (Hongjin) rebellion against the Mongols in the lower Yangtze region. Like the founder of the Han dynasty, he was very suspicious of the educated courtiers around him and was extremely authoritarian. (He became known as the "Tyrant of Nanjing.") This harsh governmental style was partly a carry-over from the previous Mongol period, which was marked by a strong centralization of governmental institutions. The Ming armies pushed back the Mongols to their original territories and rushed into Inner Asia to occupy territories that had been Chinese prefectures since the Han dynasty. Zhu Yuanzhang captured Nanjing in 1355 and took the title of emperor 13 years later. His fourth son, Zhu Di, consolidated the Ming empire, and by 1421 China was the largest nation on earth.

The Ming dynasty was famous for the influence of the eunuchs on political affairs. Trusted with performing tasks within the imperial household, many eunuchs were able to climb the social ladder and to occupy posts at the court that enabled them to influence the ruler and his decisions. Ming authority was demonstrated most significantly by the expeditions of the 15th century, led by the eunuch General Zheng He. In order to signal his power to the world, Zhu Di ordered the construction of the most impressive ocean-going fleet in history. He commissioned over 250 leviathan nine-mast treasure ships, so called because of their ability to carry vast quantities of goods. In addition, his men built 1,350 patrol ships, 400 warships, and another 400 cargo ships that would transport water, grain, and horses for the fleet.

In 1405, Emperor Zhu Di sent Zheng He on voyages to both near and distant lands. The "Grand Eunuch," as he was called, guided 27,000 people on a fleet of more than 200 boats. These were missions whose objective was to dazzle and intimidate foreign rulers, and to draw them into the "tribute system" by which rulers paid tribute to China in exchange for trading privileges and protection. These rulers were given gifts in the form of precious stones, ivory, and dyestuffs, and were offered China's treasures— mainly silk and porcelain—at a discount. As a result, they remained indebted to China. By 1433, Zheng He had been on seven voyages, visited more than 30 Asian and African countries, and brought back rare animals—such as the giraffe, lion, ostrich, and leopard—for the emperor. As a commercial (as opposed to military) strategy for world domination, it was unheard of at the time, and unmatched in its conception and execution.[9]

Emperor Zhu Di was an ambitious ruler. When he relocated his capital from Nanjing to what is today Beijing, he demolished Kublai Khan's royal palace and created a far more impressive imperial complex, the Forbidden City. Once more, to stamp his authority, he deemed that it be 1,500 times larger than the walled city of London at the time, and be home to 50 times the population. His three architects—Hsu Tai, Yuan An, and Feng Chiao—were given the brief to build an extravagant set of palaces to serve as the emperor's metropolis. Audience halls were built for receiving delegations, together with temples for ritual purification and processional paths. Within the complex were large domestic quarters, with gardens for the emperor and his family, as well as administrative accommodation, a shrine for ancestral rites, and, as patron of three types of religion, temples devoted to Buddhism, Lamaism, and Taoism. Construction took 15 years and employed the work of 100,000 skilled artisans and up to a million laborers. The grand terraces and large stone carvings were made of stone from quarries near Beijing. The floors of the major halls were paved with "golden bricks" baked with clay from six counties of Suzhou prefecture. Tragically, in May 1421, fire destroyed three main halls of the palace, including the emperor's throne. What we see today of the Forbidden City was built later by the Qing emperors, though most of the interior pavings predate the fire.

The Beijing of Zhu Di was no mere architectural wonder. In 1404, the emperor launched *Yongle Dadian*, a project to collate and preserve all the scholarly work known at the time. Under the leadership of Yao Guang Xiao and Lui Chi'ih, a team of over 2,000 scholars compiled an encyclopedia comprising 11,000 volumes. Beijing was by now an intellectual paradise, and with the mastery of printing technology, hundreds of different novels became available in its markets. Drawn by these riches and lured by the emperor's lavish hospitality, envoys from foreign lands flooded into the city and began kowtowing to China's dominant position.

It was during the Ming dynasty that the Great Wall of China became the world's largest military defense structure. In c. 220 BC, under Qin Shi Huang, sections of earlier fortifications had been joined together to form a united defense system against invasions from the north, but the wall assumed its current proportions in the Ming era. The Great Wall concept was revived following the Ming army's defeat by the Mongols in the Battle of Tumu in 1449. The Ming had failed to gain a clear upper-hand over the Mongols after successive battles, and the drawn-out conflict was taking a toll on the empire. The Ming adopted a new strategy to keep the Mongols out by constructing walls along the northern border of China. Acknowledging the Mongol control established in the Ordos Desert, the wall followed the desert's southern edge.

The Great Wall's historic and strategic importance is matched only by its architectural significance. The Ming construction was stronger and more elaborate than the earlier Qin fortifications, due to the use of bricks and stone instead of rammed earth. As Mongol raids continued periodically over the years, the Ming devoted considerable resources to repairing and reinforcing the walls. Sections near the imperial capital of Beijing were especially strengthened. Toward the end of the Ming dynasty, the Great Wall helped defend the empire against the Manchu invasions that began in around 1600.

In the midst of such grandiose expeditions and innovation in domination strategies, design flourished on a much more personal scale. One of the areas where it did so was in furniture design. By the 12th century, it had become rare in China to sit on the floor. Unlike in other Asian countries where that custom continued, the chair, or more commonly the stool, was used in the vast majority of houses throughout the country. Over the next few centuries, furniture design and construction continued to be refined, leading up to the late Ming era, which is considered by most to be the golden age of Chinese furniture. By this time, China—particularly its coastal cities—had become extremely prosperous, and the demand for luxury items—including fine furniture—had grown.

The hallmark of the Ming style was an appreciation of nature. Ming furniture brought nature into an urban setting by stressing its rhythmic pulse. The furniture of this era displayed simple, elegant lines, beautiful curves, and superb craftsmanship. For the homes of the wealthy, the wood used was hard, chosen for the pattern of the grain and the translucency of color; the material used in commoners' homes was softer, yet durable. The simplicity of their construction gave the pieces a combination of seeming weight-lessness and substance. The quality and accuracy of joinery was so precise that nails and glue were used only as supplements. Metalwork items such as handles, hinges, and lock plates were designed to complement the graceful lines of each piece. These were no longer simply functional pieces of furniture but had become objects of beauty, and their timeless simplicity remains coveted in modern times.

Which brings us back to Ming-era pottery. The Ming potters were boldly innovative, using copper oxide to produce the first red-glazed ceramics. But the most spectacular expression of the esthetic revolution was the new blue-and-white porcelain. It is not just the color scheme, with no real precedent in China, that distinguished it from the past; the handling of the clear-cut, large motifs that covered the entire available surface was evidence of the impact of the recent exposure to other cultures. The word characterizing the blue was *huihui*, a qualifier originally referring to the Iranians. The inscriptions on blue-and-white porcelain were either religious maxims in Arabic, including Koranic quotes, or Persian verses.

The time-honored Chinese high-shouldered vase, *meiping*, was interpreted in blue-and-white porcelain. For example, a vase could be decorated with a parrot perched on a prune branch, a motif borrowed from classical Song painting, while the floral border at the bottom and an Islamic geometric repeat pattern at the top would be innovations that would have startled Song connoisseurs.

Under the Xuande emperor (1426–35), Chinese potters created a type of work so difficult to execute that only four or five pieces have survived. On a dish held in the British Museum collection in London, two tones of pale brown are used on an off-white ground for a composition of sprays. The object ranks among the great masterpieces of Chinese ceramics. On another dish, the same sprays in white reversed out of blue ground create a radically different effect but betray the same love of well-delineated shapes enhanced by color contrast. The dish is one of the gems of the genre.[10]

The search for a sculptural effect culminated in the second half of the 15th century. Vases of the *meiping* type, squat wine jars, and other models were decorated with patterns suggestive of chased metal. The palette associates deep blue, turquoise, and pale yellow. A *meiping* painted with a stylized stream and riverside blossoms on a deep blue ground is probably the most powerful of all in the British Museum's collection. Simulated garlands of beads and pearls indicate that some wares may have been jeweled—actually hung with strings of pearls retaining polychrome pendants.

The Ming dynasty was overthrown by the ethnic minority Manchus over a series of battles fought between 1582 and 1644, when the Qing (meaning "clear," or "pellucid") dynasty finally took over control of China. The name "Qing" was chosen in reaction to that of the Ming dynasty, which consists of the Chinese characters for "sun" and "moon," which are associated with the fire element. The character "Qing" is composed of the water radical and the character for "blue-green," which are both associated with the water element. This name change, or "rebranding" as we would call it in contemporary times, went a long way to rehabilitate the Manchu state in the eyes of the Ming-era Han Chinese. In October 1644, Emperor Shunzi was sworn in as the ruler of a unified China at the Forbidden City. The power of the Qing dynasty would decline by the mid-19th century, and this was the last imperial dynasty before China became a republic in 1911.

The Qing emperors embellished the imperial palace with stunning craftsmanship. Every surface was decorated with bright colors and rich textures. Since the Manchus were Buddhists, the décor was strongly influenced by the paintings and designs of the Buddhist temples. In many ways, the Qing era was the antithesis of the Ming era it succeeded. If the Ming was classical, the Qing was baroque, or rococo. It was also the period when the West began to know China better. The style and esthetics of the Qing were what Westerners think of as Chinese, what the Chinese themselves believe is Chinese.[11] The architect Calvin Tsao said in an interview with Vivienne Tam, the fashion designer, "Things were much louder in Qing because they wanted to let people know who they were. But the two sides coexist...this philosophy of conservation generated so much style. All of these generations were conserving their resources and being very simple, elegant, and quiet. Suddenly, in the Qing, everything just turned around. It's a yin-yang thing, always a swing between extremes."

Vase with design of Liu Bei's wedding, Qing dynasty

Artistically, the most important emperors of the Qing dynasty were Kangxi (1662–1722), his son Yongzheng (1723–35), and his grandson Qianlong (1736–95). Emperor Kangxi consolidated the Qing state militarily and politically, and was the longest-ruling regent in Chinese history. He adapted his administration to the Confucian traditions of his dominant subjects whom he ruled for over 60 years, the full cycle of the Chinese calendar. In addition, he was a master of Han Chinese culture, including calligraphy, as well as an interlocutor of the Westerners who visited and worked at his imperial court. Kangxi's son Yinzhen, who became Emperor Yongzheng in 1723, was renowned as a great administrator who implemented fiscal and administrative reforms. His short reign was famous for the production of refined decorative arts in the palace workshops. Emperor Qianlong assembled the largest art collection in history and authored some 30,000 poems.

The arts of the Qing court—painting, silk weaving, porcelain, jade, bronzes, and lacquer—were used by the Qing emperors to express and maintain their command of the diverse territories they ruled. In their formal ritual portraits, the emperors are depicted seated on dragon thrones and dressed in ceremonial robes of embroidered yellow silk. Court robes worn by the emperors, a carved lacquer throne and screen, incense burners, and metalwork cranes are arranged in a formal court setting typical of the Qing dynasty. Cranes are the symbols of long life, and the word for "crane" is a homonym for the word meaning "harmonious." Hanging scrolls, hand scrolls, and albums show imperial palaces, hunting exhibitions to the north, and the long journeys undertaken by the emperors Kangxi and Qianlong to southern China.

Revolving vase with fencai design, Qing dynasty

Being outsiders themselves, the Qing rulers were open to Western style and influence, and the Jesuits who came to China to convert the population to Christianity were installed in the imperial court as astronomers, architects, and painters. One of the most famous Jesuits was the court artist Lang Shining, known by his Western name of Giuseppe Castiglione (1688–1766). Castiglione's paintings depicted nature in a detailed, naturalistic manner, but it is the portraits inspired by his style that are most interesting. He ran a studio in the Qing palace where imperial artists learned Western painting techniques. The fusion of Chinese and European painting styles was a key factor that defined the Qing's court painting style—an almost scientific attention to detail. The gowns they painted were rich in color, with writhing dragons and geometric patterns; the headpieces worn by the women are as elaborate as the pearls and kingfisher feathers are sensuous.

Emperor Qianlong was an art connoisseur, and he particularly loved paintings of tribute horses—symbolic gifts to the emperor from conquered nations. Qianlong was as much a skilled equestrian as an aesthete, and he commissioned individual portraits of his horses. Castiglione so pleased the emperor that the latter put his official seal on the paintings and composed a short poem praising the horses' "dragon-like" qualities.[12]

China's greatest novel, *The Dream of the Red Chamber*, was written by Cao Xueqin in the middle of Emperor Qianlong's reign. At its core, it is a simple love story wherein the fate of its hero, Jia Baoyu, is closely intertwined with the lives of two young women, Xue Baochai and Lin Daiyu. With the wealthy Jia family as the backdrop, Jia Baoyu—who is in love with Lin Daiyu—is tricked into marrying the wealthier Xue Baochai. This trickery leads to Lin Daiyu's death, and Jia Baoyu abandons his wife and the riches to seek out the life of a pilgrim. Apart from this basic plot, *The Dream of the Red Chamber* is about the quest for identity and an understanding of the human condition. It seeks the different levels of reality and illusion that lie within success and failure in life.

In the 55th year of the reign of Emperor Qianlong, the four big opera troupes from Anhui province entered the capital and combined with the *Kunqu, Yiyang, Hanju*, and *Luantan* operas popular in Beijing's theatrical circle at that time. Through a period of more than half a century of combination and integration of various kinds of operatic forms, there evolved the present Peking opera, whose richness of repertoire, multitudes of artists, size and diversity of audiences, and profound influence on cultural history and storytelling are incomparable in China. Replete with Chinese cultural facts, the opera presents the audience with an encyclopedia of Chinese culture, as well as unfolding stories, beautiful paintings, exquisite costumes, graceful gestures, and martial arts. The Peking opera is a synthesis of stylized action, singing, dialogue and mime, acrobatic fighting, and dancing to represent a story or depict various characters and their feelings of anger, sorrow, happiness, surprise, and fear. In the Peking opera, there are four main types of roles: *sheng* (male), *dan* (young female), *jing* (painted face, male), and *chou* (clown, male or female). The characters may be loyal or treacherous, beautiful or ugly, good or bad, their images being vividly manifested. The stories of the Peking opera are mainly centered around mythical tales of preceding dynasties, important historical events, emperors, ministers and generals, geniuses and great beauties, from the ancient times to the Qing era. The Peking opera's impact on contemporary creativity in China can be gauged from the fact that not only are 10-hour performances still being staged today, but also fashion designers such as Wang Xinyuan and artists such as Zhang Tiemei, who create stunning, unconventional styles, seek inspiration from the opera.

In the late 18th century, China began to dominate world trade. The rapidly growing demand for Chinese tea, porcelain, silk, and decorative pieces wasn't matched by any great demand in China for Western goods such as cotton, wool, clocks, tin, and lead. This situation resulted in a serious balance of payments problem—pretty similar to what we see between the United States and China today. Westerners had to pay for Chinese goods in silver, and this became a source of worry. One of the most significant attacks on the kingdom came from the British, who were by now on a mission to colonize and subjugate the world. The British East India Company shipped tons of opium from India into Canton (now Guangzhou), which it traded for Chinese-manufactured goods and tea.[13]

The Qing dynasty began to decline during the reign of the Empress Dowager. Its government was located in Beijing (then known as Peking), in the north, too far away to control the merchants who smuggled opium into China from the south. This trade produced, quite literally, a country filled with drug addicts, as opium parlors proliferated throughout China in the early part of the 19th century. By 1820, enough opium was coming into China to sustain the habits of a million addicts. This trafficking, it should be stressed, was a criminal activity after 1836, but the British traders generously bribed officials in Canton in order to keep the opium traffic flowing. The effects on Chinese society were devastating. In fact, there are few periods in Chinese history that approach the early 19th century in terms of pure human misery and tragedy.

The First Opium War broke out in November 1839 when Chinese junks attempted to turn back English merchant vessels. Although this was a low-level conflict, it inspired the English to send warships in June 1840. The Chinese, with old-style weapons and artillery, were no match for the British gunships, which ranged up and down the coast shooting at forts and fighting on land. The Chinese were equally unprepared for the technological superiority of the British land armies, and suffered continual defeats. Finally, in 1842, the Chinese were forced to agree to an ignominious peace under the Treaty of Nanking. The treaty imposed on the Chinese was weighted entirely to the British side. Its first and fundamental demand was for British "extraterritoriality"; all British citizens would be subjected to British, not Chinese, law if they committed a crime on Chinese soil. The British would no longer have to pay tribute to the imperial administration in order to trade with China, and they gained five open ports for British trade: Canton, Shanghai, Fuzhou, Ningbo, and Amoy. No restrictions were placed on British trade and, as a consequence, the opium trade more than doubled within three decades.

The stage had been set to benumb an entire civilization. After centuries of splendid achievement and innovation, China, in spite of never having been colonized, began to slide into disorder. Adam Smith, in *The Wealth of Nations*, argued that "China, long one of the richest, that is, one of the most fertile, best cultivated, most industrious and most populous countries of the world, had reached that stage where it had acquired that full complement of riches which the nature of its laws and institutions permit it to acquire." The growing population put new pressures on the land. The educated elite found it difficult to find employment. The enormous bureaucracy swelled its own ranks and began siphoning off government money to their own benefit—and alienating the workers who they were supposed to pay. Some of these workers began forming their own associations to tyrannize local farmers and protect their own jobs. Private interests began encroaching upon one-time government spheres, and the imperial throne could no longer assert its power.

Against this backdrop of fear and hostility, a new force began to emerge in China. It may have had different forms, but they could be encompassed by the term "nationalism"—a new awareness of identity, formed in relation—or even in opposition—to foreign forces. It embodied a sense of the Chinese people as a unit that had to be mobilized for their own survival.

A new republic was about to be born.

---

1   http://en.wikipedia.org/wiki/I_Ching.

2   *The Analects*, VII. 1.

3   www.chinavista.com/experience/shijing/shijing.html.

4   http://en.wikipedia.org/wiki/Sima_Qian.

5   Joshua Hough, "History of Chinese Calligraphy," www.art-virtue.com/history/index.htm.

6   *Drinking Alone with the Moon: The Selected Poems of Li Po*, translated by David Hinton (New York: New Directions Books, 1996).

7   Robert Payne, *The White Pony: An Anthology of Chinese Poetry* (New York: Mentor Books, 1974).

8   Theobald Ulrich, "China Knowledge: A Universal Guide for China Studies," www.chinaknowledge.de/History/Song/song-tech.html.

9   For a more complete account of Zheng He's expeditions, see Gavin Menzies' magnum opus, *1421—The Year China Discovered the World* (London: Bantam Books, 2002).

10 Jessica Harrison-Hall, *Ming Ceramics in the British Museum* (London: British Museum Press, November 2001).

11 Vivienne Tam, *China Chic* (New York: HarperCollins, 2000).

12 Lauren Arnold and Elizabeth Corsi, "Of the Mind and the Eye —Jesuit Artists in the Forbidden City in the 17th and 18th Centuries," *Pacific Rim Report*, 27, April 2003.

13 Jonathan D. Spence, *The Search for Modern China* (New York: W.W. Norton & Company, 1999).

Republic, Revolution, Reform

How 20th-century political change influenced Chinese creativity

"All our literature and art are for the masses of the people, and in the first place for the workers, peasants and soldiers, they are created for the workers, peasants, and soldiers and for their use."

Chairman Mao

Jackie Chan rubs shoulders
with Chairman Mao,
quite literally.
Moganshan Lu, Shanghai

Between 1912, when the last emperor of the Qing dynasty, Pu Yi, abdicated, and 1978, when Deng Xiaoping embarked on his program of economic reforms, China went through one of the most turbulent phases in its history. Because China was by now integrated into the world, most foreigners' impressions are based on the events that took place during this period. Notable among them was the Cultural Revolution, which spanned the decade from the mid-1960s to the mid-1970s.

When Pu Yi abdicated, China was in disarray. The nation was in deep debt, scholars and bureaucrats were unhappy with the now defunct regime, and the army had divided loyalties. At the same time, there was a transformation brought about by the development of industry, communications, and transportation. During this period of intellectual self-scrutiny and political insecurity, a group of Chinese thinkers began exploring the possibilities of progress that seemed to characterize the West. The May Fourth thinkers, as they were called, influenced by Soviet agents, were attracted to the doctrine of Marxist socialism. The movement, which grew out of a student uprising, attacked Confucianism, promoted science, and initiated a vernacular style of writing. By 1920, the group had formed the nucleus of the Chinese Communist Party. At the same time, Sun Yat-sen, the leader of the Revolutionary Alliance, who played a crucial role in ending the Qing empire, sought the release of China from the economic stranglehold imposed by the West and Japan. These Nationalists saw China shed its "feudal" past and adopt a new level of development that avoided the ills of the capitalist system. Out of a shared hope and a shared desperation was born an alliance between the Communists and the Nationalists—the desperation was over China's weak, fragmented condition; the hope lay in the spirit and intellectual power of the people to be able to coalesce into a strong nation once again. The alliance was, however, short-lived, as the Nationalists managed to outmaneuver the Communists and drove them into the rural areas.

During this time, as Chiang Kai-shek and his Kuomintang Party assumed power, urban China was transformed, with the West playing a major role. The United States and Germany provided money and skilled personnel. Roads and railways were built, as were new hospitals, schools, and colleges. Power stations began generating electricity, and cinemas became part of urban life. Wealthy homes displayed gramophones and radios; men wore suits, and women short skirts and heels. Popular artists became celebrities, and sexually explicit advertising began appearing in magazines. Smoking cigarettes became commonplace.[1] Life was good.

But there was trouble afoot. In their enthusiasm to adopt the changes, the Kuomintang neglected rural China. Population growth, primitive farming techniques, and soil nutrient depletion created poverty in China's villages. Greedy landlords, in their enthusiasm to please the foreign imperialists, began exploiting the peasants. In 1931, a devastating flood along the Yangtze River created 14 million refugees. Rural China gradually aligned itself with the Communists. And then Japan attacked China—annexing Manchuria, seizing parts of Shandong, besieging Nanking and raping hundreds of women, and eventually annexing all of eastern China from Manchuria to Fujian. By 1938, China was a divided nation. The northwest was controlled by the Chinese Communist Party, the southwest by the Kuomintang, and the east by the Japanese. It took World War II to end the Japanese domination, but meanwhile, change was brewing in the countryside.

Mao Zedong was born in 1893, into a farming family in Hunan province. As a young man, he served in the local student volunteer force in Changsha. Rebelling against his father, rejecting the marriage arranged for him to the daughter of a neighbor's family, Mao immersed himself in study. By the time he was accepted as a student of ethics at the First Normal School in Changsha, he had studied John Stuart Mill, Rousseau, Spencer, and Montesquieu, as well as many Chinese political philosophers. His formal study introduced him to the works of Kant. Mao's initial analysis of China's weakness was literal—China was weak because the Chinese were weak, physically. It was because their culture emphasized building up the mind over building up the body. In the spring of 1930, Mao embarked on a meticulous study of the conditions in rural Jianxi province, looking for the prevalent levels of exploitation and analyzing class tension. In doing so, he recognized the special needs of women, influenced by one of his Changsha friends, Xiang Jingyu, who had been active in the fight for women's rights and socialism. One of Mao's early writings was about the suicide of one Miss Zhao: "it happened because of the shameful system of arranged marriages, because of the darkness of the social system, the negation of individual will, and the absence of the freedom to choose one's own mate." When Mao later took control of Jianxi province, he promulgated a new marriage law that prohibited arranged marriages and encouraged the free choice of spouses. He also recognized that women among the poorer classes had more say and greater power than did those among the upper classes. Even as Mao played a dominant role in Jiangxi—one that had attracted attention because of his presence—it was not the only rural communist enclave. At least a dozen regions were holding out against the Kuomintang. In 1934, Chiang Kai-shek launched an economic blockade and encircled Jiangxi with his troops. Faced with annihilation or attempting a next-to-impossible escape, the Communists chose the latter. The breakout, which began under the cover of darkness on October 16, 1934, is considered one of the most heroic events in history. The Long March, as it is called, ended with the communist forces victorious after trekking across almost 10,000 kilometers over 370 days.

By 1945, near the end of World War II and the Japanese withdrawal, the Chinese Communist Party had 1.2 million members. Mao's leadership of the party was undisputed. The influence of the Kuomintang was on the wane, and Chiang Kai-shek retreated to Taiwan, as a final stronghold for his party, when the Japanese left the island. Chiang was succeeded by Li Zongren in January 1949, but not for long. The Communists gave him an ultimatum; when he refused to accept it, they overran Nanking, Hangzhou, and Wuhan unopposed, Shanghai with a token resistance, and soon Canton, Xiamen, and Xinjiang. On October 1, 1949, Mao Zedong stood at the Gate of Heavenly Peace in Beijing and announced the birth of the People's Republic of China.

In the early 1950s, Mao led a massive economic and social reconstruction that was generally welcomed by a population desperately longing for stability. The Communist Party gained popular support by curbing inflation, restoring the economy, and rebuilding many war-damaged industrial installations. To lead the social revolution, the party, which had legitimized itself into the guiding force of socialist China, extended its rank-and-file to all Chinese regions and set up various institutions to lead changes in rural areas, the military, and the bureaucracy. Landmark changes in the early 1950s included the adoption of the Gregorian calendar and the abolition of political-era names, the embedding of women's rights into law and the abolition of polygamy, and the adoption of a horizontal left-to-right method of writing.

Mao's success lay in his adaptation of Karl Marx's communist theories, based on highly industrialized economies, to the conditions of an agricultural society. Land reform was the major focus of policy as a result of China's vast rural population. (Around 90% of the population were farmers.) Land owned by former landlords was confiscated by the government and subsequently redistributed to the lower-class peasants between 1950 and 1953. Mao wiped out the old landlord class, and gradually equalized the wealth gap in the remaining classes. Immediately following the land reform period came the Three-Anti and Five-Anti movements, as well as the beginning of the Anti-Rightist Movement, when property owners and businesspeople were labeled as "rightists" and purged. Some scholars put the number of those killed during this period at a million or more. Rural China, however, achieved a quasi-classless system that ultimately disbanded the imperial feudalism that was the norm of dynastic rule. Major public health institutions sprang up in both urban and rural communities, as both agriculture and industry experienced significant growth between 1949 and 1958.

Mao's social and cultural programs, including collectivization, were mostly popular in the early 1950s. However, China's strained relations with the new Soviet leader Nikita Khrushchev and newfound contradictions between the Chinese and Soviet schools of communism seeded a novel and radical drive to reform China's economic system in its entirety. Mao broke with the Soviet model and announced a new economic program, the Great Leap Forward, in 1958, aimed at rapidly raising industrial and agricultural production. Ambitiously, Mao announced the goal of surpassing the steel production output of Great Britain by 1968. Giant cooperatives, otherwise known as people's communes, were formed. Within a year, almost all Chinese villages were reformed into working communes comprised of several thousand people who would live and work together as envisioned by an ideal Marxist society. "Backyard factories" producing useless steel dotted the Chinese landscape and became a hallmark of the period.[2]

The results were disastrous. Agricultural production fell behind, normal market mechanisms were disrupted, and the Chinese people exhausted themselves producing what turned out to be shoddy, unmarketable goods. Because of the reliance on the government providing and distributing food and resources and their rapid depletion due to poor planning, starvation appeared even in fertile agricultural areas. In 1960–61, the combination of poor planning during the Great Leap Forward, political movements incited by the government, and unusual weather patterns and natural disasters resulted in widespread famine. The death toll was between 20 and 40 million. The disaster of the Great Leap Forward decreased Mao's stature as national leader and even more so as an economic planner. After he was criticized within the Central Committee during this period, President Liu Shaoqi and Party General Secretary Deng Xiaoping took over the party and launched pragmatic economic policies that went against Mao's communitarian vision. They disbanded the communes, in an attempt to restore the system to pre-Leap standards. Unhappy with mainland China's new direction and his own reduced authority, and apprehensive that his legacy may lie in shambles after seeing Khrushchev's demise, Mao launched a massive political attack on Liu, Deng, and other pragmatists in the spring of 1966. The new movement, termed the "Great Proletarian Cultural Revolution," was in theory an extension of the class struggles that hadn't been completed during the last revolution.

Between 1966 and 1968, Mao's principal lieutenants and his wife Jiang Qing, acting on his instructions, organized a mass youth militia called the "Red Guards." The aim was to overthrow Mao's perceived enemies and seize control of the state and party apparatus, replacing the Central Committee with the Cultural Revolution Committee, and local governments with Revolutionary Committees. The thoughts of Chairman Mao became the central operative guide to all things in China. The authority of the Red Guards surpassed that of the army, local police authorities, and the law in general. China's traditional arts and ideas were ignored, with praise for Mao being practiced in their place. People were encouraged to criticize cultural institutions and to question their parents and teachers, which had been strictly forbidden in Confucian culture.

The Cultural Revolution was a hyper-multimedia production, long before these words became part of our daily vocabulary. Extending far beyond the posters, the messages of the Cultural

Revolution saturated every type of medium available. The reproduction of words and symbols—through radio and television, theater and art, books and pamphlets, postcards and collectors' cards, ornaments and badges—intensified the impact of the Cultural Revolution. At mass assemblies in Beijing's Tiananmen Square, people held up their copies of *Quotations of Chairman Mao*, the same red book portrayed on posters, postage stamps, and alarm clocks. Citizens recited together from their books at study meetings, and covered their physical surroundings with the quotations so that buildings, walls, and natural features all proclaimed the thoughts of Mao Zedong. Ceramics factories turned their energies to producing statues of characters from revolutionary musicals (the so-called "model works"), the same characters portrayed in posters of the time. Art and literature workers "transplanted" entire musical texts from one genre to another, and detached individual pieces from song and dance dramas to be sung in rallies and chimed on clock towers. This monumental web of texts, images, sounds, and movements surrounded and caught up Cultural Revolution participants and bystanders alike.

As a participatory event, the Cultural Revolution was meant to move people both emotionally and physically. As in previous 20th-century political movements, the performing arts proved to be particularly effective in encouraging participation. Music coordinated the actions of the masses in a very real sense. People rhythmically waved their red books and marched together to music, singing "with one voice." Wherever they might be—in dining halls, on trains, in schools, and at work in the factories and fields—Chinese citizens heard the same music broadcast over public loudspeakers. Repeated and performed daily, the music was familiar to people from all walks of life and from all parts of the country. We often hear that the music of the Cultural Revolution was monolithic—that people were allowed to perform only the same "eight model operas" throughout the period. While this characterization is partly true, only a few years into the Cultural Revolution, 18 works were officially designated as models; and these models were constantly revised and transplanted into different formats. Apart from these models, many other compositions based on Mao's words were produced and reproduced.[3]

The music encompassed a variety of styles, including those from Chinese traditional music (a term usually used to refer to styles of music developed in China prior to the 20th century). It also incorporated instruments and harmonies associated with Europe and the West. From the 1930s through the 1950s, art and literature workers devoted much of their creative energies to producing compositions based on Chinese folk music. But by the late 1960s, the direction of their work had shifted when Jiang Qing decided that she did not like "vulgar" folk songs. Being labeled "incorrect" wasn't necessarily the end of the line for a musical composition, however, since some pieces could be "revised," just as some people of suspect political character could be "re-educated." Collectives of art and literature workers, "with assistance from the masses," revised and adapted pre-existing works and composed new ones. A set of strict, albeit changing, principles guided their production. To keep track of the changing guidelines, circulars printed directives on cultural work and newspapers printed commentaries on recent productions.

One early revolutionary song, "The East is Red," survived throughout the entire period, becoming the substitute national anthem of the Cultural Revolution when the national anthem of the PRC was condemned because its lyrics were written by Tian Han, who was branded as a counterrevolutionary at that time. "The East is Red" was written in the 1940s by a poor peasant living near the communist base area of Yan'an, where Mao resided. It began:

> The East is red, the sun has risen.
> China has produced a Mao Zedong.
> He works for the people's happiness;
> He is the people's savior.

It became the title song to the *East is Red Song and Dance Epic,* performed in Beijing by 3,000 workers, peasants, students, and soldiers in 1964 in celebration of the 15th anniversary of the People's Republic of China and released as a film. The piece musically dramatized the story of Chinese revolutionary struggle in the first half of the 20th century and included some of the best-known revolutionary songs from the period.

The army revolutionary song "The Three Rules of Discipline and the Eight Points of Attention" stood second in importance to "The East is Red" during the Cultural Revolution. The three rules were: obey orders; don't take a needle or piece of thread from the masses; and turn in captured goods and do everything to ease the burden of the people. And the eight points of attention were: speak politely; pay fairly; return things you borrow; pay for things you damage; don't hit or swear at people; don't damage crops; don't take liberties with women; and don't mistreat captives. The goal was to elevate the soldiers of the Red Army to the status of role models, and the model works often emphasized the close relationship between the Red Army and the Chinese people.

The well-known composer Xian Xinghai (1905–45) wrote and revised his massive *Yellow River Cantata* during the war period (1939 and 1941). The Yellow River constituted a persistent theme of revolutionary music, often serving as a metaphor for China and its beauty and hardships. Set to words by Guang Weiran, the piece called the compatriots to war to recover the homeland from Japanese occupation. Xian Xinghai, officially called the "People's Composer," used folk songs or work songs from the masses in many of his compositions. The cantata formed the basis for the *Yellow River Piano Concerto* adapted during the Cultural Revolution by noted pianist Yin Chenzhong and others. The concerto soon took its place among the model works. By the clever act of hauling his piano into the fields and playing revolutionary songs for the masses, Yin established the "bourgeois" piano as an instrument acceptable within the musical pantheon of the Cultural Revolution and established himself as a revolutionary musician.

Politically, having a large cult of personality put in place, Mao emphasized the "destruction of the Four Olds," a radical renunciation of old norms and feudal traditions, and denunciation of all ideologies deemed to be counterrevolutionary, including Confucianism, imperial tradition, superstitions from folk religion, beliefs of ethnic minorities, and organized religion. Education at all levels was brought to a virtual halt as Mao launched another phase in the Down to the Countryside Movement, where young urban intellectuals would be sent down to the countryside to learn from the peasants. The university entrance examinations came to a complete halt, and most high schools closed. Religious and educational institutions were big targets. Nuns, priests, monks, authors, teachers, professors, and artists were beaten, publicly humiliated, or forced to kill themselves. China shut itself off from the world, and the Bamboo Curtain came up.

The tragic paradox that underlined the Cultural Revolution was that greater political equality, in the context of an overwhelming emphasis on ideological conformity (*yiyuanhua*), ultimately resulted not in expanded freedom of expression but in its sharp curtailment. The Cultural Revolution had been expected to bring greater freedom, but its actual consequences were just the contrary. The attempt to transform everyday practice to conform with ideological precepts had its most telling impact on routine meeting behavior and on workaday participation in the economy. In both realms, the impact was to promote more exacting conformity with prescribed routines.

The Cultural Revolution was characterized by conformity that was as much symbolic as ideological. The popularity of the Mao suit provides an illustration of the prevailing conformist mentality of the era. The roots of the Mao suit can be traced back to Sun Yat-sen and the Nationalist government. In an attempt to find a style of clothing that suited modern sensibilities without completely adopting Western styles, Sun Yat-sen developed a suit that combined aspects of military uniforms, student uniforms, and Western-style suits. In the late 1920s, civil servants of the Nationalist government were required by to wear the Sun Yat-sen suit, which would later be called the Mao suit. After the Communist Revolution, the Mao suit became a symbol of proletarian unity and was regularly worn by party cadres. Political leaders were not the only ones to wear Mao suits. People of both genders, in all parts of the country, and in all kinds of professions, began wearing variations on the suit on a daily basis. In a number of practices the Communist Party strived to minimize social differences, and this egalitarian approach was perhaps given its most noted application in the elimination of insignia in the ranks of the People's Liberation Army in 1965. Many women felt that a return to the restrictive clothing of the upper classes in China would be a retrogressive step. They saw their present mode of dress as a symbol of their emancipation.

As the Cultural Revolution spun out of control and grew past Mao's original intentions, his ability to control the situation—and, in turn, his authority—dwindled. By 1969, the Red Guard organizations were disbanded. After the infamous Lin Biao incident,[4] many of the officials who had been criticized and dismissed during 1966–69 were reinstated. Chief among these was Deng Xiaoping, who re-emerged in 1973 and was confirmed in 1975 in the concurrent posts of Politburo Standing Committee member, People's Liberation Army chief of staff, and Executive Vice-Premier in charge of the State Council's daily workings.

In focus group discussions, that we conducted, Chinese men and women repeatedly named Deng Xiaoping when asked to nominate a very creative person. It was a clear recognition of Deng's ability to outmaneuver the system, even as he was so much a part of it, in pursuit of his vision.

Deng was born in 1904 in Paifang village, Sichuan province. His father, Deng Wenming, was a wealthy landlord—later dispossessed of his land—who owned a house with 22 rooms and sent his son to study in France at the age of 16. Working first at the Le Creusot Iron and Steel plant in central France, then as a fitter in the Renault factory in the Paris suburb of Billancourt, later as a fireman on a locomotive and as a kitchen helper in restaurants, young Deng came into contact with his senior Zhou Enlai, and was introduced to Marxism. He joined the Chinese Communist Youth League in Europe in 1922, and traveled to Moscow. In 1927, he returned to China, led the failed Baise Uprising in Guangxi province against the Kuomintang government, and arrived at Mao's Jianxi province, joining the latter on the Long March and becoming one of his trusted supporters until Mao grew wary and purged him from positions of power. After Mao's death, Deng carefully mobilized his supporters within the Chinese Communist Party, and was able to outmaneuver Mao's anointed successor, Hua Guofeng, who had previously pardoned him, and then ousted Hua from his top leadership positions by 1980–81.

Deng made it on to the cover of *Time* magazine, as "Man of the Year," in 1978. In January 1979, four weeks after the resumption of China's diplomatic ties with the United States, he visited America for a week. The most lasting image from that trip was of the diminutive Deng wearing a 10-gallon hat. Soaking in American culture by touring the Ford factory in Atlanta, trying his hand at the space shuttle simulator in Houston, and meeting the Harlem Globetrotters, Deng became America's favorite Communist. He declared, "To get rich is glorious." The Bamboo Curtain was about to part.

Deng set about charting the path for China, and the Chinese, to get rich. He laid down the principles for Chinese economic thought—socialism with Chinese characteristics, which consists of mixed forms of private and public ownership competing within a market environment, creating a system that is in essence identical to capitalism but where the state dominates parts of the economy. In a speech to a Japanese delegation at the second session of the Council of Sino-Japanese Non-Governmental Persons on June 30, 1984, Deng pronounced:

> The fundamental task for the socialist stage is to develop the productive forces. The superiority of the socialist system is demonstrated, in the final analysis, by faster and greater development of those forces than under the capitalist system. As they develop, the people's material and cultural life will constantly improve. One of our shortcomings after the founding of the People's Republic was that we didn't pay enough attention to developing the productive forces. Socialism means eliminating poverty. Pauperism is not socialism, still less communism. The present world is open. One important reason for China's backwardness after the industrial revolution in Western countries was its closed-door policy. After the founding of the People's Republic we were blockaded by others, so the country remained virtually closed, which created difficulties for us. The experience of the past 30 or so years has demonstrated that a closed-door policy would hinder construction and inhibit development. We are suggesting that we should develop rapidly, but not too rapidly because that would be unrealistic. To do this, we have to invigorate the domestic economy and open to the outside world.

Our socialist economic base is so huge that it can absorb tens and hundreds of billions of dollars worth of foreign funds without being shaken. Foreign investment will doubtless serve as a major supplement in the building of socialism in our country. And as things stand now, that supplement is indispensable. Naturally, some problems will arise in the wake of foreign investment. But its negative impact will be far less significant than the positive use we can make of it to accelerate our development. It may entail a slight risk, but not much.

We shall accumulate new experience and try new solutions as new problems arise. In general, we believe that the course we have chosen, which we call building socialism with Chinese characteristics, is the right one.[5]

About 30 years ago, Shenzhen consisted of not much more than paddy fields. Then, in May 1984, Deng turned Shenzhen into a Special Economic Zone (SEZ), the first of several—Zhuhai and Shantou in Guangdong, and Xiamen in Fujian—that would follow. The location was chosen to attract foreign investment, especially industrial investment from Hong Kong, since the two places were near each other and shared the same culture. Being in the Pearl River Delta, the access to a large port would be key to its success. There were other strategic reasons for the choice of Shenzhen. The old guard in the Chinese Communist Party were still present and watching Deng's every move carefully. Deng figured that Shenzhen, far from Beijing, would not be on their radar. If he failed, few would notice. Should he succeed, he could use the model and replicate it elsewhere. The chief economic decision-maker in China at the time, Chen Yun, remarked: "It is necessary to establish special economic zones, but such experience needs to be reviewed from time to time, if the zones are to be developed successfully."[6]

In setting up the Shenzhen SEZ, it was hoped that by attracting capital investment initially from Hong Kong and Macau, rather than multinational capital, international capital would follow suit after seeing the evidence of a successful capitalist operation. When China implemented its "open door" policy in the 1980s, Hong Kong's manufacturers were already seeking to shift a large portion of their production offshore, with a view to escaping the rising labor costs. As a result, much of the machinery that was virtually obsolete in Hong Kong was transported across the canal that forms the northern boundary of Hong Kong's New Territories and put into operation in Shenzhen. Most of the initial infrastructure for the SEZ was internally financed through down payments by the newly formed joint-venture enterprises (JVEs) for land-use rights and other imposts. As a result of massive investment in construction in 1982, industrial output value rose dramatically.

The outsourcing of the labor-intensive operations associated with Hong Kong's manufacturing activities added substantially to the capacity of the colony to continue exporting manufactured goods, and gave rise to exports of semi-finished products and components from Shenzhen into Hong Kong. The success of these ventures soon became apparent to multinational enterprises in other countries, and they also formed joint ventures in Shenzhen. Many of these were brokered by Hong Kong's financial institutions and were assisted by other service establishments there. As a result, Hong Kong's services sector grew at a much faster rate than manufacturing, especially after a greater proportion of the total product was manufactured in Shenzhen.

During Shenzhen SEZ's first five or six years, most of the labor supply was obtained through migrant workers who fulfilled short-term contracts and then returned to their home towns and villages. The wage rates in Shenzhen were substantially lower than in Hong Kong, but were well above the rates that prevailed in the migrant workers' towns and villages. The workforce needed by the JVEs was therefore met by young Chinese who sought increased savings within a relatively short period of time.

Over these years, Shenzhen has enjoyed an annual average growth rate of 28%. Today it contributes US$35 billion in net exports to the Chinese economy. Fourteen percent of China's total exports come from Shenzhen alone. Looking down on the world's sixth-busiest port today, one sees an ocean of 100,000 shipping containers, each about the size of a semi-trailer truck, stacked eight high like 40-foot-long steel Legos. They carry garments, furniture, and the latest high-tech gadgetry, more than half bound for the United States. The dockyards of Shenzhen are a steel-and-concrete testament to the velocity of China's emergence as a free-trade titan. The Las Vegas-like city has wide boulevards, muscular marble-and-glass office towers, glitzy stores, and cascades of neon advertising. Downtown pulsates day and night. The popular theme park Window of the World has about 130 reproductions of some of the most famous tourist attractions in the world squeezed into 480,000 square meters. The Eiffel Tower, at 108 meters (354 feet), dominates the skyline, and you can pack in the Pyramids, Angkor Wat, the Taj Mahal, Niagara Falls, and the Lincoln Memorial in half a day.

At Lotus Hill Park, local residents have their photographs taken in front of Deng's statue. "Without Deng, there would be no Shenzhen," they say in gratitude. It is a sentiment echoed everywhere: without Deng, there would be no modern China. And modern China is being propelled by creativity.

---

[1] Jonathan D. Spence, *The Search for Modern China* (New York: W.W. Norton & Company, 1999).

[2] http://en.wikipedia.org/wiki/History_of_the_Peoples_Republic_of_China.

[3] www.sino.uni-heidelberg.de/conf/propaganda/musik.html.

[4] At odds with Mao, Lin Biao attempted to stage a military coup in September 1971. When the coup failed, he tried to escape to Russia, but his plane came down in Mongolia, apparently shot down.

[5] www.wellesley.edu/Polisci/wj/China/Deng/Building.htm.

[6] James Kung Kai-sing, "The Origins and Performance of China's Special Economic Zones," *Asian Journal of Public Administration*, 18(1), June 1996.

From Pianos to Postmodern Punk
The ferment in contemporary music in China

"Suddenly there was an opportunity
Everything was empty, we had no goal
Just like when our mothers gave birth
And we weren't consulted at all
What could this opportunity be in the end
We still haven't thought about it too clearly
But events have already rushed out of control, seriously."

Cui Jian, *"Touji Fenzi."* Translation by Andrew Jones

Zhang Fan and Cui Jian
in conversation
(Courtesy Zhang Fan)

When Tong Zhi Cheng started working at Pearl River Piano in 1959, three years after the company had been set up in Guangdong province, he was just 16-years-old. The factory had dirt floors. "We rented a shed on the side of the street to repair pianos, and we built a shelter to process the wood. It was very, very small. I still remember we used a cart to carry the piano and we walked barefoot to the port. That's how we exported at that time,"[1] remembers Cheng. Pearl River was, and remains, a state-owned enterprise. Cheng rose to head the company by 1995. Today, it is the world's largest piano manufacturer, with the capacity to make 100,000 pianos a year. The factory covers 310,000 square meters and has 4,000 employees. Robert Witmeyer of San Jose Piano in California says, "In the history of mankind there probably hasn't been as good an entry-level piano."[2] Pearl River's success has come from focusing on quality and aiming for the masses, but forging alliances with Yamaha and Steinway has enabled the company to creep slowly up the value chain.

Eighty percent of Pearl River's sales come from China itself. With 30 million students learning to play the piano (and 10 million playing the violin), that's not surprising. Virtuoso performers such as the pianist Lang Lang don't come along every day, but if even 10% of China's student pianists prove to be truly gifted one can imagine the impact they might have on the world of Western classical music. In April 2007, the *New York Times* carried an article headlined "Classical music looks toward China with hope." Chen Hungkuan, chairman of the piano department at the Shanghai Conservatory, is quoted as saying: "[Classical] music is hot in China. It may be fading in Western countries, but in China the talent is unlimited." Chinese children are being pushed to study an instrument, both as a possible means of advancement in the country's supremely competitive school system and as a way of providing a well-rounded education. Greater prosperity means that more families can pay for lessons, which has made it possible for former government employees such as Chen Yuanyuan, in Lanzhou, to give up their jobs and earn far more by giving private music lessons.

So, where does this fascination and interest come from? Is it the rigid rules of Western classical music that the Chinese are instinctively attracted to, or is it the opportunity for stardom in a society where individuals are hungry to be recognized? To answer this question, we must go back in time and attempt to understand the interplays that have determined the creative direction of music in contemporary China.

China's musical tradition goes back some 3,000 years and has a distinctive sound—originating from gongs, cymbals, plucked lutes, and zithers. It lacks the bass and tenor sounds of many Western instruments, while the singing is high-pitched and nasal. One of the oldest instruments is the six-stringed zither, or *guqin*, which the Chinese literati considered to be the most refined of instruments. The *guqin* has no bridges; the large vibrating amplitude and rich low tones are perfect for conveying the sounds of nature. In ancient China, the *guqin* was played at small, intimate gatherings. Legend has it that Yu Boya, a *guqin* player in the Spring and Autumn Period (770–476 BC), performed only for his woodsman friend Zhong Ziqi, who appreciated the instrument's spiritual nature. When Zhong Ziqi died, Yu destroyed his *guqin* because he believed no one else could appreciate and understand his music. Playing the *guqin* was considered to be one of the four arts of the Chinese scholarly class (*qi*—chess, *shu*—calligraphy, and *hua*—painting, being the other three). This elitism remains evident today. Gong Yi, China's leading contemporary *guqin* player, has commented: "Many *guqin* players look down upon musicians playing other Chinese instruments. They limit themselves to a small circle and indulge in playing dozens of old pieces, never thinking of how to develop the *guqin* to modern times. Why not play to an audience of 1,000?" Gong Yi has no such problem, playing to packed houses at the Shanghai Oriental Arts Center and the Golden Concert Hall in Vienna alike.

Baibai plays the guqin in Linxia

Although prototypes of the *pipa*, or the four-stringed lute, existed during the Qin dynasty (221–206 BC), the modern-day instrument traces its origins to the Persian *barbat*, which found its way to China during the Jin era (AD 265–420) and achieved immense popularity during the Tang dynasty (618–907), when it was played in the imperial court. It had a crooked neck, four or five silk strings, and five or six frets, and was played with a plectrum in a horizontal position. Over the centuries, the number of frets increased to 24, the neck became straight, playing with a plectrum was replaced by playing with the fingers, and the practice of playing the instrument while holding it vertically became commonplace. *Pipa*-playing Buddhist deities are depicted in the wall paintings of the Mogao Caves near Dunhuang. The instrument is also referred to frequently in Tang dynasty poetry, where it is often praised for its refinement and delicacy of tone.

Unlike the *guqin*, over time the *pipa* achieved greater popularity and its sounds underwent significant experimentation. In the early and mid-20th century, two of the most prominent *pipa* players were Sun Yude (1904–81) and Li Tingsong (1906–76). Both were active in establishing and promoting *guoyue* (literally "national music"), a combination of traditional regional music and Western musical practices.

In the late 20th century, largely through the efforts of Wu Man, Min Xiaofen, and other performers, Chinese and Western contemporary composers began to create new works for the *pipa*, both solo and in combination with chamber ensembles and orchestras. The *pipa* has also been used in rock music; for instance, the California-based band Incubus featured it in their song "Aqueous Transmission," played by guitarist Mike Einziger. Lin Di, of the Shanghai-based progressive folk/rock band Cold Fairyland, also plays the *pipa* as a centerpiece of the band's act.

The *erhu*, or two-stringed bowed fiddle, on the other hand, emerged from a folk tradition. Introduced into central China by minority tribes during the Tang dynasty, it is often found in Chinese folk operas and ballad forms as a background instrument used to suggest pathos. It was also traditionally played at ceremonies such as weddings and funerals. The modern *erhu* dates back nearly 100 years, to when Liu Tianhua (1895–1932) composed the first solo piece for the instrument, "The Sound of Agony," in 1915. Xing Liyuan, a contemporary exponent of the instrument, says: "The famous composition '*Jiang He Shui*' ('River Water') sounds like a woman's wailing. Once I played '*Er Quan Ying Yue*' ('Moon Reflects over the Second Spring') and a neighbor's boy came over and asked, 'Who is crying here?'"[4]

European classical music had long, if not deep, roots in China and has been associated with modernity for centuries. The Jesuit Matteo Ricci brought with him a clavichord when he visited China in the late 16th century. An Italian missionary, Teodoricus Pedrini, arrived in Beijing in 1711 and wrote court music for Emperor Kangxi. At the turn of the 20th century, China's middle class turned to European sounds as the music of the future. It was a quirky musical path. The piano repertoire, comprising sonatas and variations, was alien to the evocative tradition of Chinese instrumentalism. The piano was expensive, and beyond the means of most Chinese families. But therein lay its attraction: it was seen by the modernizers as the ideal vehicle for musical progress.

Virtually unknown outside China, Xian Xinghai, the composer of *Yellow River Cantata* (mentioned in the preceding chapter), was one of the most famous composers of the 20th century. Xian belonged to a poor family and encountered much hardship in his early years. He made his way to Paris by undertaking an arduous journey as a stowaway to Singapore, where friends and relatives helped him buy a ticket to France. Trained at the Paris Conservatory, he was struck by the crowds of marchers singing "*La Marseillaise*" on Bastille Day, and came to believe that the primary function of music was to rouse the masses to revolutionary activism. Upon his return to China, he began composing "mass songs" that were sung in chorus, or to the accompaniment of Western instruments such as the piano or the accordion. His supreme achievement came with the *Yellow River Cantata*. When Mao heard the first performance of the cantata, he signaled his enthusiasm by sending the composer a bottle of ink and a fountain pen. Xian Xinghai was admitted to the Communist Party. In 1940, at Mao's bidding, he went to Moscow to compose the music for a group of Soviet filmmakers who were making a documentary entitled *The Eighth Route Army and the People*. By the time Xian died in 1945, he had become a romantic hero, especially among the Chinese middle class—in the tradition of Western composers such as Chopin, Schubert, and Mozart.

If the piano survived the attack on most things Western during the Cultural Revolution, it was due to the efforts of Yin Chenzhong.[5] From being a target of the revolution, it came to be a positive symbol of radical change. Yin was born in 1941 on Gulangyu Island, a charming enclave of Xiamen, in Fujian province. Home to many foreigners, Gulangyu had a flourishing musical tradition. Unlike Xian Xinghai, Yin was born into a prosperous family and began taking piano lessons at age seven. Five years later, he was sent to study at the Shanghai Conservatory, where he began receiving his musical education from Chinese teachers as well as those from the Soviet Union. At the age of 19, he won first prize at the World Youth Festival held in Vienna, and traveled to Leningrad to study at the conservatory there. He took second place at the Tchaikovsky Competition, playing a combination of Western pieces and a Chinese suite written by Du Mingxin and Wu Zuqiang from the ballet *The Mermaid*. He returned to China as a hero, giving concerts in Shanghai and Beijing, and continuing to perform in Leningrad and Moscow despite mounting tensions between China and the Soviets. But as the Cultural Revolution began to take effect, artists came under attack. Among Yin's contemporaries, female pianist Gu Shengying was forced to kill herself, Fou Ts'ong went into exile, and Liu Shikun was placed under arrest.

Yin responded in one of the smartest ways possible—exhibiting one of the hallmarks of the creative instinct. Fond of Chinese opera, he began composing new pieces that would be symbolic of Chinese culture, such as "The Fishing People Sing of the Communist Party" and "*Yangge* Dance." He made his home among farmers near Beijing. Even as the Red Guards began smashing pianos in homes and locking up conservatories, Yin was able to enthuse peasants about his music. He took the piano, that erstwhile instrument of the concert hall and drawing rooms, to the streets. Loading it on the back of a truck, Yin, along with members of the Central Philharmonic Propaganda Team—mostly rebels under pressure to prove themselves as revolutionaries—arrived at Tiananmen Square on May 12, 1967, for a rally. Yin played revolutionary songs such as "The Peasant Congress has Convened" and "Long Life to Chairman Mao" for the Red Guards that day, and returned the next to play Jiang Qing's favorite symphony, *Shajiabang*. He then toured army bases, factories, and nearby villages. As the demands to eradicate the piano continued among the radical Communists, Yin created the opera *The Red Lantern*, which tells the story of a railway worker, Li Yuhe, who sent secret messages during the Japanese occupation. The opera premiered at Beijing's Great Hall of the People on July 1, 1968, and Chairman Mao, Zhou Enlai, and Jiang Qing posed for photographs with him and other performers. Yin was declared a national hero. It was a classic case of surviving adversity, and then using it to further one's individual creative goals.

A pianist performs at Super Brand Mall in Shanghai

Music, then, became a refuge for many. Musical talent was one of the few things that could offer an escape from being sent to carry out hard labor in the countryside, where millions of urban youth were sent to commune with the peasants. Inspired by Yin, thousands of young men and women who knew how to play Western musical instruments joined the revolution's song-and-dance troupes. "Every kid—if you had 10 fingers, you were playing something at that time," said Li-Kuo Chang, the Chinese-born assistant principal violinist of the Chicago Symphony Orchestra. "Whether you had talent or not, that was a way of saving you [from being] sent to the factory or farm." By 1972, violins were in short supply.

No longer. In the small studios and shops on leafy Fuxing Road in Shanghai's French Concession, shop-owners can be seen polishing and tuning up their stringed instruments, while others sell sheet music. There are an estimated 1,000 violin-makers in China today, churning out 250,000 of the instruments every year. It is a mere 50-year-old industry, and profitable indeed. Zheng Quan, one of the country's foremost violin-makers, sells his sonorous pieces—he has made only 70 so far—for US$10,000 each. He won the Stradivarius Competition for the best-sounding violin, held in Cremona, Italy, in 1991.

Lang Lang is an able successor to Yin Chenzhong's legacy. Inspired at age three to learn the piano after watching the cat Tom giving a piano recital in "The Cat Concerto" episode of the *Tom and Jerry* cartoon series, the piano prodigy went on to win the Tchaikovsky Competition at age 13. Now in his mid-twenties, he has been a top-class professional pianist since the age of 15. He played solo at Carnegie Hall in New York at 21, has performed at the White House in Washington, DC and at the headquarters of the European Union, and gives 150 performances a year. In an act of sheer boldness, he invited his father—his teacher when he was very young—to join him onstage at Carnegie Hall and accompany him on the violin for the finale. The two played a Chinese piece. CBS news hailed Lang Lang as "maybe the best of his generation." He has been interviewed by Jay Leno and has performed on *Sesame Street*. Part MTV rock star, part Mozart, he is being counted upon by his recording company, Deutsche Grammophon, to bring many more young fans into the fold of classical music. Lang Lang hasn't disappointed them—reaching No. 20 on Billboard's New Artist charts. And that wasn't the classical music charts, where his recordings of Beethoven's Piano concertos No. 1 and 4 went straight to the top in May 2007.

Steinway & Sons recognized the inevitable business opportunity in Lang Lang's popularity, especially in China. In March 2007, even as he was being recruited by UNICEF as its goodwill ambassador, Steinway launched the "Lang Lang" line of pianos. It was the first time the company had named a piano after a living artist. Priced at a fraction of what a Steinway costs in the West, no doubt to capture the market in China, the piano's design elements include a reversible front panel that converts into a whiteboard, and a music desk that runs nearly the length of the keyboard to make musical scores easier to read.

Nearly 2,000 miles northwest of Shanghai lies Lanzhou, a dusty city of three-and-a-half million. It is the geographic center of China. One would imagine that the fascination for Western classical music would ebb as one went further into China's heartland, but nothing could be further from the truth.

Chen Yuanyuan performing the Peking Opera at age seven

In Lanzhou, we were warmly welcomed into the home of Chen Yuanyuan. Chen grew up learning the Peking opera. He showed us black-and-white photographs of his first performance at the age of five. He was admitted to the Xi'an Music Institution to learn the cello in 1978, when the Chinese government reopened the universities after 10 years of the Cultural Revolution. When he was 16, he joined the Communist Youth League, and soon after began playing the cello at state functions. Finding it difficult to survive as a cello teacher within the government establishment, Chen broke away in the early 1990s. He began teaching young students on his own, and playing in bars, clubs, opening ceremonies of business establishments, and wedding parties. He and his radio disc jockey wife now own a duplex apartment, complete with a *mahjong* room to entertain their friends and, of course, a music room.

Dudu playing the cello at her home in Lanzhou

Chen's daughter Dudu is his favorite student. She obliged us by playing a Dvorak piece. Fluent in English, unlike her parents, she touts cellist Yo-Yo Ma as her idol. She dreams of winning a scholarship to one of the famous music academies, and understands that it is only by working hard that she will be able to realize her dream.

If Chen Yuanyuan is playing his part in passing on a Western classical tradition in Lanzhou, Chengdu in southwestern China is rapidly emerging as a center for indie Chinese rock. The owner of The Little Bar, Tang Jie, is referred to as the "mother of rock music" in Chengdu. The bar is, as its name suggests, quite small, but it regularly packs in over 150 people standing shoulder-to-shoulder for its Friday night rock and punk shows. Mid-afternoon, the third and top floors hum in anticipation of the coming night's events. Cameramen and girls mill about as the bands do their sound checks. The sun filters through the tobacco and weed smoke. Two very young girls sell beer, T-shirts, and CDs. "This is definitely underground," says Tai Ran, lead singer of Ashura, a prominent Chengdu band freshly signed to a Beijing label. "This concert has no official recognition, no permission, and no big sponsors—man, we came here on the bus." The underground music scene used to thrive in Chengdu's bars in the form of house bands. No longer.

Hitting the right notes at Nanluoguxiang hutong, Beijing

The same group of once-underground artists that helped create The Little Bar just before the turn of the century now drives BMWs and Hummers around town. Their work is lapped up by the Europeans, especially the French. They make frequent visits to Beijing and Tibet: to the former to solidify their ties to the above-ground; to the latter to re-establish ties to their roots. Tibet is "cool"; Beijing is necessary. Tai Ran's definition of underground transcends borders: broke and illegal, down-to-earth, and creative. "The road toward 'above-ground' is paved with the souls of the creative," he says.[6]

Big-time multinational firms, and the consulates that represent them, are steadily tapping into the growing pool of musicians and DJs to promote their products and their culture. The Canadian Consulate-sponsored Mutek Festival held in March 2005 featured a long list of bands and DJs and visited every major city in China.

The big liquor companies—Coors, Carlsberg, Chivas, Heineken, Absolut—are using every tool at their disposal to break into one of the biggest guzzling markets on the planet. Pretty peasant girls in tight skirts and shiny brand-name outfits patrol the KTV bars and clubs, promoting Chivas and green tea and Carlsberg Chill. Skyy Vodka has an army of girls following the waitresses around. But these girls can only sell so much. Now these companies—and other giants such as China Mobile, Sony, Siemens, etc.—are creating acts and taking the west of the country—Lanzhou, Gansu province, Xian, Chongqing, and Kunming—by storm.

It is a world that has evolved quite significantly from the idealism and heroism of the first generation of China's rock musicians. The first rock band in China, Wan Li Ma Wang, performed covers of Western rock when it launched in 1980; another band, Alisi, performed Japanese songs. Then arrived Cui Jian, commonly referred to as the "godfather of Chinese rock." For him, rock music had meaning and a message. It had to function as a cultural force that inspired social change. At the very least, it had to make people think. Cui Jian was well-read, and both Chinese and Western philosophers, such as Nietzsche, Schopenhauer, and Sartre, influenced his thinking. In 1986, his song "*Yi Wu Suo You*" ("Nothing to My Name") became an instant hit, one of the most popular songs in Chinese music history. To a generation numbed by the deadening propaganda of the Cultural Revolution, the honesty of Cui Jian's lyrics was like a clarion call.

> I've asked tirelessly, when will you go with me?
> But you just always laugh at my having nothing
> I've given you my dreams, given you my freedom
> But you always just laugh at my having nothing
> Oh! When will you go with me?
> Oh! When will you go with me?
> The earth under my feet is on the move
> The water by my side is flowing on
> But you always just laugh at my having nothing
> Why haven't you laughed your fill
> Why will I always search?
> Could it be that before you I will always have nothing?
> Oh! When will you go with me?
> Oh! When will you go with me?[7]

Cui Jian kept a low profile for many years. Then, on September 24, 2005, he once again emerged in Beijing with his loud and angry wall of sound in his first officially sanctioned concert in the capital in 12 years. Some 10,000 fans gathered to hear the star perform at a concert entitled *A Dream in the Sunshine*, held in the Capital Gymnasium. The fire still burned within, but Cui Jian had mellowed. In an interview with the UCLA Asia Arts Institute, he seemed to have veered away from his anti-establishment roots, and struck a conciliatory note. "Rock music is more personal to me. I have more freedom. For the next generation, I think there is a lot of good stuff in the arts. But what is good art? I'm sure it means freedom and creativity…I want Chinese people to have a chance to create and explain themselves more and see what is the difference."[8] He lamented the commercialization of the music industry. "All artists listen to the seller. They don't listen to their managers or the producers. They don't listen to themselves…They are controlled by the sellers."

Rock band Maya belts it out at Nanluoguxiang hutong in Beijing

From the early 1990s, Chinese musicians began to absorb influences from a range of genres and ideologies. The new generation of musicians were financially comfortable, having either jobs or the support of their families. They no longer propagated rock music as a liberalizing force. Rather, they composed and performed within a new, negotiated cultural, economic, and socio-political space. The focus shifted from words to sounds. The realm of experimentation moved into combining the old with the new. The counterculture spirit of punk took on an entirely new dimension. Describing the punk phenomenon, Jin Wang writes:

> The general consensus is that Chinese punk is a fashion accessory for hip kids. Although they are considered avant-garde among the young generation, their expression is far from being radical. It is an opportunistic trend born from the restless, upstart mentality of the sons and daughters of the middle class. Deep in their blood, Chinese punkers are neither rebels nor extreme fun-seekers. They are "potbellies"…living a lifestyle of leisure and safe boundaries, marked by insatiable desire for fame and money.[9]

While that may be the case, it is also true that punk musicians and their fans express their feelings in reaction to something. For many, it is a reaction to the oppressive education system, exemplified by the college entrance examinations, or *gaokao*. For a period in their lives, these young men and women are driven by a desire to turn that world upside down. Music that offers total disjunction and delivers rapture appeals to them. But it is a short-lived phase. Once they cross this hurdle, many college students switch their loyalty to "cool" pop singers from Taiwan, Korea, and Hong Kong. The transition from the Re-TROS and *Cangying Yuedui* ("The Fly") to Faye Wong, Teresa Teng, and Jay Chou is quick.

The record label Modern Sky in Beijing, and music aficionados –event promoters Yuyintang in Shanghai, understand this evolution and recognize the range of music styles prevalent in contemporary China. They realize that, to be commercially viable, their recordings, collaborations, and events must span genres.

Artist, designer, entrepreneur, sometime lead singer of the funk-pop band Sober (*Qingxing*) Shen Lihui set up Modern Sky Entertainment in 1997. The record label produces music content across the genres of rock, pop, world music, electronica, dance, and jazz—bringing out about 15 titles a year. They have their own chain of independent music stores, and an office in New York. Modern Sky maintains close relationships with foreign music content providers such as EMI, Pias, Beggars Group, Cooking Vinyl, Gronland, and G-Pop through both the exclusive licensing of foreign music for China and the export of Chinese music to the world. In the face of free music downloads, and pessimism on the part of Tower Records and Virgin Music ("We cannot think of opening a store in China, not just yet," said Richard Branson), it has become the most successful music company in mainland China. Modern Sky's graphic design group, Money Design, is the brains and brawn behind Modern Sky album art, posters, and ads for the music releases. The design team works on open, unfettered briefs, and creates some of the most exciting album art seen in China. It also designs album covers for other performers who are not under the Modern Sky label. Subsidiary company Modern Sky Digital Entertainment, formed in 2005, creates and distributes a wide variety of creative, innovative music and animation content for both wireless and Web platforms.

The two faces of Shen Lihui: entrepreneur and rock star
(Courtesy Shen Lihui)

Modern Sky's pop music label M2 releases albums by singers such as Chang Kuan (*Never Say Goodbye*) and Guo Jieming. The former sold 300,000 copies and is one of the biggest-selling albums in China). Guava, the chill-out–lounge music label, provides a platform for musicians from Tibet to cut new CDs. While we toured the premises, an album of Tibetan rock was being sampled. Shen Lihui explained: "*Touch Tibet* is the most widely released album for Modern Sky. It has been published in Europe, Japan, Malaysia, and other countries. It was a very important album for Modern Sky. We wanted to see if it would sell at a very high price, RMB160 [around US$20], and it did." But Shen has now moved those sounds to the World Music label. He went on, "Our staff took all the recording equipment to Tibet and stayed there for three weeks. We collected all the material—including the deep chants from the Buddhist temples—and are combining it with modern instruments. This will be a regular plan. We'd like to dig music in Tibet, Yunnan, and pay attention to how folk music is combined with other types of music."

The Badhead label focuses on what Shen describes as underground music, "in order to provide the new generation with a means of articulation." Bands such as Joyside have released albums titled *Drunk is Beautiful* and *Bitches of Rock 'n' Roll* under the label, belting out furious pieces such as "Loser's Face," "Music Sucks," "(I am) Lazy and Wasted," "I Wanna Piss on You," "Univershitty," and "I Don't Care About Society." Re-TROS, a tight postmodern punk trio we heard performing at Yuyintang Warehouse, ramps up the sentiment. "This country is run by monkeys," they let blast in their song "Hang the Police."

With grit like that, it is no small wonder that many companies shy away from associating themselves with such music and such bands. Shen sounded rather despondent. "The recording part of my business isn't a profitable venture. I do it because I love this music so much." He is able to indulge his passion for one simple reason: the commercial application and potential of the music. Only, this music is different. Modern Digital works with clients such as Motorola, Nokia, Carlsberg, Levi's, and Audi to create a wide range of entertainment properties, ranging from screensavers to ringtones to Web-based games, organizing college music contests, identifying the right music for the brands to sponsor (such as lounge music for Carlsberg), and holding music festivals. They launched the Modern Sky–Apple iPod® Shuffle Special Edition, as their music became available in the iTunes® store. As music itself evolves to seek multiple responses—and to play an ever-larger role in contemporary lives, as our companion, reminder, wallpaper, provoker, relaxant… the list continues to increase—companies such as Modern Sky have successfully adapted themselves creatively to face the future, and sometimes lead us to it.

Tucked away in a warehouse district on Long Cao Road in Shanghai, a small black door framed by a mural was a beguiling invitation to Yuyintang. Piercing guitar riffs escaped into the street; the Re-TROS were tuning up for the show. We had an appointment with the band's PR/marketing manager, Joecy Wu. Chairs were set out on the deserted street; it was too loud to have a conversation inside. And she began to recount their tale.

In 2004, five former high-school friends got together and decided to do something about their shared passion for rock music. Finding time outside their day jobs, they began inviting rock bands to stage shows in Shanghai—at first, in clubs and bars. As more people began to come to the shows, they were able to raise enough money to rent a warehouse and to buy some good sound equipment and instruments. Joecy said, "Yuyintang believes that rock music brings young people a sense of rebellion, enthusiasm, and creativity, which is the most needed spirit of China's contemporary youth. Only with such a spirit can Chinese youth think independently and experience their own lives." We waited to hear the band perform, to find out if the act reflects Yuyintang's values.

We asked Joecy if finding regular sponsors was a problem. The entrance fee for that night's performance was only RMB30 (around US$4), and the warehouse could accommodate only about 250 people standing. The band wasn't going to get rich off the door takings, we commented. Joecy shrugged. "As you probably know, Shanghainese are more into jazz than rock." I had been guilty of paying RMB280 to see Salena Jones perform for 3,000 enthralled fans at the hip, huge Shanghai Oriental Arts Center. Cadillac had sponsored the entire event, including plying 100 or so journalists with wine. "We approached Heineken once," Joecy said. "They said, 'We get 20 sponsorship requests a month.'"

The band finished their sound check and we went inside. A small space was plastered with posters of performances that Yuyintang had organized. The first, held in 2004, was a tribute to John Lennon. The travails of convincing a bar in fashionable Xintiandi to let them play, discovering that not many youngsters were happy to fork out RMB40 for a rum and cola, convinced them that they had to find their own space.

Some friends painted murals on the warehouse walls, and other photographer friends exhibited their photos of the Shanghai rock scene. Zhang Haisheng, one of the founders of Yuyintang, joined our conversation. "Rockers in China have limited exposure," he said. "Unless you're exposed to a variety of styles, musicians, and their work, you can't create new stuff. We don't get many international bands—the Rolling Stones don't count; they are over—*well over*—the hill. Only those under 35, those who grew up after China opened up, value creativity. Our friends and colleagues envy us and think what we are doing is really cool and helps us realize our own dreams, but our parents think we spend too much time outside our daytime job, which isn't a good thing." We asked him which bands were known for their originality. "Cold Fairyland," he replied. The band's bassist, Su Yong, was at the bar and agreed to an interview after the show. Integrating the sounds of the traditional *erhu* and the *pipa* with guitars, synthesizers, and drums, Cold Fairyland has been described as one of the most creative bands in the mainland. I was eager to hear their version of The Beatles' "Eleanor Rigby."

The audience began to arrive, mostly college students and fresh graduates in their early twenties and a few expatriates, probably drawn by the listing in *That's Shanghai*. A policeman popped his head inside, asked a few questions, and then left. "The police don't trust any gathering of young people," Joecy explained. I don't know if any money changed hands.

Couples snuggled in the corners; Tsingtao and Budweiser beers were lapped up at the bar. My colleagues Jane and Kate struck up a conversation with some of the audience. "Are you here for work?" they were asked. "You don't look like punk rock fans!" We didn't look the part, evidently, and the dress code was an important part of the experience.

Formed in 2003 by singer–guitarist Dong Hua, singer–bassist Min Liu, and drummer Hui Ma, Re-TROS (also known as Re-establishing the Rights of Statues) quickly became one of Beijing's hottest bands. The lights were turned down, and the band kicked up the tempo with its opening song. The audience went delirious, screaming and jumping around. One track flowed effortlessly into another. The lyrics were bold; the track "TV Show (Hang the Police)" began with: "Hang the police under his shotgun, Hang the police before we are all murdered." Thankfully, the man in uniform had already left.

Simplification best describes the Re-TROS' brand of post-punk, reminiscent of late 1970s David Bowie with elements of Joy Division. On their album *Cut-Off!*, the trio delivers six tracks running 30 minutes: tight, straightforward guitar riffs, unfussy base lines, and solid drumming. Minimalism, however, didn't necessarily mean minimal quality.

Indeed, the band's meticulously polished sound owed a lot to Brian Eno, who was acknowledged on the CD jacket. While on a visit to China, the legendary producer of David Bowie, U2, and Depeche Mode added color and texture to the Beijing band's sound and even mixed in some keyboard on a couple of tracks. Nor, for that matter, were the English lyrics simple. Indeed, each song told a different story. "If the Monkey Becomes the King" referred to the famous novel *Journey to the West* while alluding to the stupidity of humankind.

> Oh if the monkey becomes (to be) the king, is it so crazy?
> They kill your men, your women, your children, your futures, your minds, your bodies and your music
> This country belongs to the monkey.[10]

Yuyintang's next act was AK-47, who play "new industrial metal." A flyer described them thus: "They are fierce and full of rage; but lyrics cold and full of aestheticism. Their live performance is just like man-eating typhoon, demonstrating the beauty of violence all the time." It was a pitch designed to lure the young and the restless among China's youth.

Even as the warehouse filled up every weekend, there were some who weren't pleased with the sentiments the bands were arousing. On April 11, 2007, as Beijing punk band Brain Failure took to the stage and the first power chord rang out, the crowd was transformed from a silent shuffling group of people to a sweaty, mashed-up, screaming mob. In the middle of the seventh piece, a photographer climbed on stage and whispered in the guitarist's ear. The guitarist stopped playing, followed by the other band members. After a short conversation, the singer smiled wryly and put his finger to his lips.

The show had been stopped by the Xuhui District Culture Bureau. Yuyintang Warehouse was being shut down for not possessing a "performance license." Joecy would later write an e-mail to the media about the closure:

> We understand that to host performances legally, firstly, you have to apply for a performance license for the venue. This is almost impossible for us because we don't have the money and the *guanxi* to get passed [*sic*] the checks from the fire control, food control, etc. After all, we are a rock warehouse which is only open when there's a show. It's not our intention to ask people to pay a lot to see a rock concert or to spend a lot on drinks. Secondly, you have to apply to the Culture Bureau every time there's a concert. In addition to this, the artists and singers also must have a "*yan yuan zheng*" (performer license) if you want to give a charged performance according to the government's newly released guidelines. This is again, something impossible to realize. Although, we are facing a large fine from the Culture Bureau that we don't know how to deal with it at the moment, the determination to put on rock shows is firm. To all the rock believers, Yuyintang won't go away![11]

Pluckily, Yuyintang moved to a new venue—at Zhijang Dream Factory in the New Factories, on Yuyao Lu in Shanghai's Jing'an district—in June 2007.

The mantra in modern China is evidently: "creativity within boundaries." It is up to the individual to test what those boundaries are.

The band members of Cold Fairyland believe in pushing artistic boundaries, rather than political ones. On a rainy Saturday afternoon, we made our way to Su Yong's apartment, where the band was practicing a new piece. After 30 minutes of rehearsal, they were ready to talk. Lin Di, one of the founders of the band along with bassist Su Yong, cradled the *pipa* which she has been playing since she was four. Zhou Shenan, who studied at the Shanghai Opera School, plays the cello; Li Jia plays drums and is a percussionist with traditional operas; and Song Jiang is on guitar. Crammed into a tiny room overflowing with sound equipment and instruments both modern and ancient, the group seemed very much like the cradle of creativity that they are reputed to be.

Cold Fairyland performing at Yuyintang Warehouse

The band describes itself thus:

> The past, present and future of Shanghai's underground. A cold fusion of sound that brings you a melancholy single voice to tsunami's summit. Tasting its heaviest depth with the hint of metal that crashes down upon you. Combining traditional and modern instruments, armed with rock heart and the bitter taste of life, this union of skilled performers plays with the freedom of jazz soaring through the night. An atmosphere thick as honey, you can almost taste this new wrought sound.

"We named ourselves after one of Haruki Murakami's books—I like her very much. The name reflects the sometimes dark tones of our music," began Lin Di. Explaining the urban roots of their music, she said: "We were brought up in cities, so we don't have so many historical or cultural roots as our previous generations did. We are educated in the same way as many other people. We all majored in music, and there was no other option for us."

So, how did the band evolve and earn their reputation?

Lin Di explained: "In China, there are professional bands and non-professional bands. Professional ones perform in pubs every night to make money. Most of the time, they copy music and play covers. We did the same when we needed to build up our skills. Later, we realized that copying was boring, so we began creating original music. At ARK [a bar in Shanghai's Xintiandi], they offer opportunities for original music once a month—it's been going on for four years. We began performing at ARK, first half original numbers and half covers, but later only original pieces. It was quite tough. We wrote one new original song each month and had a stage to practice. We are not like many other bands whose priority is making money; doing original music is their second aim. We've done the opposite. Now if we're invited to do covers, we won't go. Previously, as long as a band can copy some music, they could earn several thousands. But it's not the case anymore. The market wants original music. We don't know exactly why the fans love our music, but they do." It is the inexplicable sense that you

Lin Di of Cold Fairyland
(Courtesy Lin Di)

have when you spot a good piece of creative work, no matter in what field.

Su Yong added, "We're a brand now. Earlier, people would only look for live bands. Now they want Cold Fairyland. We're no longer pressured by the demand for entertaining an audience or working for others. Now we can do what we like. We feel happy doing what we're doing now. If we feel painful, we'll give it up. Being happy is the first thing, but of course, if we're not profitable, do you think we'll do it?"

Cold Fairyland is driven by originality and creativity. Su Yong attempted to define creativity: "It is something new, that hasn't been done by other people before. It's also related to innovation, being ahead and trying something experimental." Li Jia chimed in: "Don't be held down by inertia, and think independently." Lin Di added: "Don't repeat yourself." Li Jia continued: "But we're sure of one thing: everybody should not be filled with pop music. They only know 'I love you, and you love me,'" taking a dig at Chinese and neighboring pop stars. Everyone laughed. "We've reached a consensus about what we don't like," summed up Su Yong.

Cold Fairyland, pre-performance

Being happy and having fun—key drivers for the creative person—seems to infuse the thoughts and actions of Wei Wei and Huang Yixin, now popularly known as the Backdorm Boys. The duo from Guangzhou, in southern China, became famous for their lip–sync videos of songs by the Backstreet Boys and other pop stars. It all began with a bit of tomfoolery by the then sculpture students. Inspired by short lip–synced videos they saw on the Internet, they decided to create one of their own. The Backstreet Boys were quite popular at the time, and their hit, "As Long As You Love Me," became the subject of their experimentation. A third dorm boy, Xiao Jing, is in the background of most of the videos. He usually plays the computer game "Counter-Strike" while Wei Wei and Huang Yixin are performing. Captured on a low-quality Web cam in their college dorm room, the boys did their first video for fun and to show their friends, who later uploaded it to the Internet —and the world took notice immediately. Many of their videos can now be seen on YouTube.

The combination of having fun with music and the power of the Web made the Backdorm Boys famous very quickly. They appeared on the *Ellen DeGeneres Show* in the United States, were signed on as spokespersons by Motorola to market their phones, by Pepsi, and by the Chinese portal Sina.com. Ogilvy, Motorola's agency in Asia, created an online lip–sync competition to promote entry-level phones, and sales zoomed by 270% in four months.

We met the duo, still exuding naïveté, in Beijing, along with their talent manager. The Backdorm Boys were quite candid about their inspiration: "Our creativity comes from a foreign video. That's it—two foreigners singing a rock song, about 40 or 50 seconds long. We felt a bit let down when it ended so quickly. So we decided to do a longer one." But it is also evident that they work in tandem, having fun and inspiring each other. Wei Wei explained: "We've lived in the same dorm for a long time and are good friends. We share a lot in common, like our hobbies. We do get funny ideas because of each other. Just look at us—we are so different physically. One is tall, the other is short. We have our personal quirks but believe in each other. So as long as we're in front of the camera, no matter what the other one is doing, we can cooperate." An art college background certainly helped them. "We were studying at art college, so we had many ideas to play around with and were in a free situation," he said.

It seems that the Backdorm Boys are on a mission. Huang Yixin explained: "We'd like to inspire everyone's entertainment cells. Get some fun through entertainment, don't be so old-fashioned, and don't lead a boring life. We want to provide everybody with a relaxing and creative new life. We'll dig out the fun and entertaining spirit from the smallest part of our lives and inspire people to do the same."

Zhang Fan gesticulating, Midi School of Music, Beijing

Playing a visionary role in China's modern music scene is Zhang Fan, headmaster of the Midi School of Music in Beijing's Haidian district. The son of university professors, he majored in trade and economy; he played the guitar from the time he was in middle school, and formed a band while at university. All quite conventional so far. In 1993, the country was just opening up. As they were exposed to new forms of music for the first time, many young people began thinking of making a career in modern music, but there was no place to learn. "Because of the market need and my own interest in music, I decided to start the school along with some friends," explained Zhang Fan. "It wasn't too tough to get it off the ground. Many students came, as we caught their eye. It wasn't just young kids who wanted to learn; there were ex-servicemen, for example. Finances were never a big problem for the school." Zhang Fan was at the right place at the right time, even as a visionary. His school focused on the basics—the artistic and humanistic theory of modern music, encompassing rock, blues, jazz, funk, Latin, pop, country, and fusion; and the practice of music technique. Enrolment soared with every passing year. "Most of the top performers and those in the music industry are graduates of the Midi School," he says proudly. The Midi School has received support from the Haidian local government, which recognizes it as a brand in the creative industry.

When the school began its extremely popular Midi Festival, the government allowed it to use a public park. Zhang Fan cited one reason for its popularity: "Our pricing of tickets was also creative. Till then, admission to any live show was very expensive. We recognized that young people couldn't spend very much. We got a beer company to sponsor the festival and served free beer. They loved it." That brought us to a discussion of the meaning and value of creativity.

According to Zhang Fan, "Creativity is an idea. If you put it in a broad way, it advocates social progress and lets common people have fun. If you put it more life-oriented, creativity satisfies your own dreams and objectives. Good creativity should serve the society as much as it should serve the artists. Our creativity lies in promoting a culture and a lifestyle. People in China like to play *mahjong* and go to karaoke bars in their spare time. There were few outdoor music activities. But in the West, outdoor music activities have thirty, or even more years of history. Midi Festival is the first ever in China. In the past seven years, there're more and more such music festivals around China. Actually it is a kind of cultural activity for common people, which I think is helpful for building a harmonious society. Nowadays, folks live in high buildings, stuck behind computer and TV screens without any communication, so we need this activity, a shared language. People come out to enjoy some sunshine on the weekend. Families or relatives and friends hang out together, drinking beer, singing and dancing, and sitting on the green grass, which is a very healthy lifestyle. I think we're doing the government a favor. People express their depression or anger in the festival. The government has recognized this and has labeled the festival a good activity where strangely dressed-up young people have fun and don't fight anymore."

Music has always played an integral part in the lives of Chinese people—from serving a ceremonial purpose, to celebrating occasions, to being a vehicle for courtship as well as dissent. Recent changes in society and technology have made the creation, participation in, and appreciation of music much more democratic, giving birth to new genres and new talent. Some will go on to achieve the fame of Lang Lang and the Backdorm Boys, some the popularity of the Midi Festival; others will merely sway to the ever-evolving beat. It is a phenomenon that typifies the creative resurgence of China.

---

[1]   www.pbs.org/nbr/site/onair/transcripts/050627_chinachange1.

[2]   Russell Flannery, "Piano Man," *Forbes*, May 13, 2002.

[3]   Michelle Qiao, "Playing the *Guqin* was Required of Literati, Nobility," *Shanghai Daily*, June 8, 2007.

[4]   Michelle Qiao, "Beauty, Passion and Special Effects," *Shanghai Daily*, June 22, 2007.

[5]   Richard Curt Kraus, *Pianos & Politics in China* (Oxford: Oxford University Press, 1989).

[6]   Sascha Matuszak, "Bumpin' it in China," www.Antiwar.com, March 21, 2005.

[7]   Cui Jian, "*Yi Wu Suo You*." Translation by Andrew Jones.

[8]   Cui Jian interviewed by Larry Kao, UCLA Asia Arts Institute, April 28, 2004.

[9]   Jin Wang, "Youth Culture, Music and Cellphone Branding in China," *Global Media and Communication*, 1(2), 1995.

[10] Liner notes: *Cut-Off*, by the Re-TROS (BadHead Records, 2006).

[11] www.smartshanghai.com/blog/721/Live_Music_:_Interview_with_Joecy_Wu_shanghai.

Million-dollar Dreams

The art market takes off

"Before, all China cared for was that people could eat and read. With the new system, socialism with a market economy, China has become more international. This is my duty as an artist in this century—to provide beauty for the people."

Chen Yifei (1946–2005)

Artist at work in Moganshan Lu, Shanghai

The year 2007 was a very good year for the art market in China. Never before had the work of so many Chinese artists fetched such high prices. In April, Sotheby's in Hong Kong sold an oil painting by Xu Beihong (1895–1953), *Put Down Your Whip*, for the equivalent of US$9.23 million. The 1932 painting depicts a young village woman, apparently pleading to be spared public humiliation, while others look on. A month later, Chen Yifei's revolution-themed *Ode to the Yellow River* was auctioned by China Guardian for US$5.16 million. Total sales at China Guardian jumped to US$77.69 million in the spring of 2007. Li Feng, director of the modern and contemporary art department at Huachen Auction Company in Beijing, is delighted. "There has never been a year with so many artists hitting personal records over US$1.3 million,"[1] he said. In late 2006, Wu Guanzhong's five-meter-wide oil painting *Ten Thousand Kilometers of Yangtze River* fetched US$4.94 million; earlier that year, Sotheby's sold *Pink Lotus*, by Chang Yu, for US$3.6 million. Zhang Xiaogang's collection of portraits and landscapes raked in over US$24 million. Between them, Sotheby's and Christie's sold RMB 1.4 billion (US$190 million) worth of Asian contemporary art in 2006, most of it from China. From having only one artist from China on their list in 2001, the number has leapt to 25. Even so, most artists remain unknown outside China, or the Chinese art collector circuit.

That's the value end of the market. At the volume end, Dafen village, a buzzing little enclave near Shenzhen, is legendary. Depending on your perspective, it is the art lover's worst nightmare, or dream come true. Some 8,000 painters—mostly young, some disabled but talented—churn out five million oil paintings a year. If you buy them by the dozen, a reproduction Van Gogh, Monet, or Gauguin can be yours for as little as RMB40 (US$5). Dafen contributes RMB500 million (US$68 million) to the Chinese economy. How did this happen?

In 1989, Hong Kong artist and budding entrepreneur Huang Jiang moved to Dafen with a plan to use the mainland's pool of low-cost painters to produce art reproductions for export. His success attracted others, and there are 600 galleries in the little village today, exporting to foreign art wholesalers, big retail chains, and individual buyers. Foreign art dealers travel to Dafen from Europe and the United States, ordering copies of famous paintings by the container load. While the paintings by European masters remain the favorite copy subject, the recent popularity of Chinese art means that more of that is being copied. "The contemporary Chinese knockoffs—retro-revolutionary Wang Guangyis, the precocious baby-populated Tang Zhizhangs, and the sneering Yue Minjuns"[2] are popular among foreigners. Increasingly, "Westerners buy the Chinese paintings, and the Chinese buy the European paintings," says one of the gallery owners. To express their gratitude, the artists and the municipal government erected a bronze statue of Leonardo da Vinci in the village square.

Huang's former student, now competitor, Wu Ruiqiu runs the company Shenzhen Artlover. He ships 300,000 paintings a year and is one of Dafen's model companies. The businessman is dreaming of industrial mass production, complete with assembly lines. The creation of every painting would be divided into standardized production stages. Ruiqiu wants to "get into the business of oil paintings the way McDonald's got into the business of fast food." He also wants to set up an art school for training talented new painters—even if mass production doesn't require all that much talent.[3] His painters make RMB1,000 (US$135) a month, or a little more, better than what many factory workers do. But thanks to the voracious appetite of art lovers in China and the West, Wu Ruiqiu has already made his first million, in dollars.

Arguably China's most successful artist commercially, within his own lifetime, Chen Yifei was born in 1946 in Zhenhai county in Zhejiang province. He moved to Shanghai when he was very young, graduating from the Shanghai Art Training School in 1965 and studying at the Shanghai Institute of Painting. Chen's talent earned him quick recognition by the political authorities, and he was commissioned to paint big portraits of Chairman Mao and grand heroic scenes of the formation of "modern China." In 1970, he was appointed the head of the oil painting department at the Shanghai Institute. As the revolution drew to an end, Chen abandoned his party glorification themes and began painting melancholic and lonely women in traditional Chinese dress, Chinese musicians playing traditional instruments, and Tibetan villagers—in the process founding the "Romantic Realism" school of Chinese painting. In 1980, he took his big chance and went to New York to work as a professional artist and to study Western art. Earning a Master's degree from Hunter College, he painted some major works, including the oversized portrait of oil tycoon Dr. Armand Hammer and *The Bridge of Peace* for the United Nations. By the 1990s, critics were unable to categorize his work. It blended Western and Eastern cultures and styles, but common to all his works was a commitment to beauty.

It was this keen eye for beauty that led Chen Yifei to admire the fashions on the streets and in the stores of New York City. Each time he returned to China during the 1980s, he would lament the lack of color. "There were a billion people living without any real sense of lifestyle," he would say. "My dream was to bring aesthetics to Chinese society." Returning to Shanghai, he founded the fashion label and lifestyle store Layefe. Soon, his empire extended to 100 stores in 35 cities, and fetched him US$25 million in revenue. And that was in addition to what he earned from his paintings. As China emerged from the "lack of color," Chen remarked: "Chinese have a lot of money now. But they need inspiration on how to spend it tastefully. That's where I come in."[4] In 1993, Chen also began making movies. His first film, *A Date with Dusk*, was entered at the Festival de Cannes. He followed it up with two artistic documentaries, depicting the experiences of Jewish people living in Shanghai during World War II. In 1995, midway through his fourth film, *The Music Box*, Chen Yifei died suddenly of a stomach haemorrhage. He was 59.

Over the last decade, the commercial rewards and fame earned by Chen Yifei, and the boom in the art market, have inspired thousands of young people to unleash their creative potential and hone their skills and imagination. China now has 20 to 30 art schools, with about 10,000 students estimated to have graduated from those schools in 2007. At the same time, dealers in art and museums are mushrooming all over the country. There are already over 3,000 art galleries in China; 300 operating in each of Beijing and Shanghai. Between them, they represent around 14,000 artists. In Shanghai, an estimated 50,000 people were engaged in the business of Chinese art and calligraphy in 2007.

The enthusiasm for art isn't confined to the big cities. For instance, Dingxi county in Gansu is home to scores of art galleries. People there are known for their passion for art and will buy paintings or other art objects whenever they have spare money. Dingxi residents are said to prefer a painting to a television set in their living rooms. And only original works are considered worth displaying.

Artists and art entrepreneurs are joining hands in making art accessible—indeed, even ubiquitous. Victoria Lu represents that sentiment. She is the creative director of the Museum of Contemporary Art (MoCA), a small but influential gallery set inside the verdant People's Park in central Shanghai. Born into a Shanghainese literati family in Taiwan, she emigrated to the United States in the early 1970s. She attended both the College of Chinese Culture in Taipei and the Academie Royale des Beaux-Arts in Brussels, but received her Bachelor and Master of Arts degrees from California State University, majoring in painting. She started writing art criticism in the mid-1970s for Taiwanese newspapers and magazines. By the end of 1978, she had begun her curatorial career, taking on the position of director/curator of the alternative space Stage One Gallery in southern California, showing mainly conceptual and installation art. Returning to Taiwan, she began helping the government to establish policies regarding public art and the promotion of art education to the general public.

Martian Aerocraft, by Tzu-hsun Lee, "Animamix" exhibition Moca, Shanghai

We met Victoria in the café atop MoCA. She had just miraculously survived her car's falling into a gorge in Yunnan province. She sported a sling, but her enthusiasm was undiminished. "You can't separate art from everyday life," she began. "If you separate art from life, it diminishes its magical power. Just look at the contrast between European art and what you see in India. In the Western European tradition, art was meant for rich people's living rooms. And a lot of sculpture was for architectural decoration. But look at India—art is everywhere, on the village walls, on the palms of women. Fabric, jewelry—it's all part of the living environment. It's fascinating. Earlier, it was only the elite, the nobility, who could enjoy art. But today, anybody can enjoy and experience art on the Internet. So, people wake up. Art is no longer reserved for a particular class. It is highly consumed by everyone in society. I don't believe in high culture—culture is for everyone."

Victoria's descriptions are metaphorical, yet accessible. "People talked about the pyramid idea in the past—there was the top class, a few, and the bottom class, the majority. I have changed the pyramid to a ball. A ball can roll; it is dynamic. Who is on top, who is at the bottom, can change. They take turns." She is also provocative, and believes strongly in the democratization of ideas. It is a strong belief, which, if considered seriously, can have significant implications for the way the creative industries are run. "I believe that knowledge belongs to the people. I mean, the copyright idea only took root in the 1970s. Before, there was no concept of copyright. So, humans shared their intelligence and used it to improve civilization. If people had to pay for knowledge and ideas, then only the rich can obtain knowledge. That's not good for society." Egging her on, I seek her opinion about the "counterfeit painters" of Dafen village. "You should thank those counterfeit factories. They sell to those who cannot afford the goods produced by the art galleries. They make only marginal profit, but they are filling up homes with art. If people want to create an aesthetic environment, why should money be a barrier? Maybe the children in those homes will buy the originals, if they become prosperous. I don't understand why people get upset."

Under her tutelage, MoCA is attempting to make art more audience-friendly. "People should come in and feel the art, interact with it. Even if they don't understand a particular piece, they can still enjoy the color, the light, the environment. Museums have to redefine themselves. I think that a theme park is the biggest installation art piece an artist can produce. It is dynamic; it is visually appealing." MoCA gives children crayons and encourages them to have a go. It is part of an interactive experience that allows people to "get into the art."

Victoria Lu isn't alone. "Get It Louder" offers people a three-dimensional experience by creating a unique media marketing platform that blends the shopping experience with exhibition-viewing. The "Get It Louder" exhibition is a new and open platform for the exchange of ideas. It is a visual chorus of the new-

Inviting children to draw at MoCA, Shanghai

generation designers, artists, and creative people; a fantastic collection of cross-media creations, ranging from print graphics to Web design, product, fashion, animation, video, architecture, multimedia installation, and sound art—almost everything. All in all, it's a passionate and lively party, a noise made on purpose. Their exhibitions don't take place in museums or art galleries, but rather in shopping malls, where large numbers of people who wouldn't normally be expected to visit galleries interact with the installations. Financially, too, their model is unconventional. Rather than make money by selling artworks, they sell advertising spaces within their exhibitions, in collaboration with the Guangzhou-based Modern Media Group. Staging the exhibition within a shopping mall gives them this latitude. It is a moving show, aiming at maximum exposure. In Guangzhou, the Grandview Plaza in Tianhe district was chosen as the venue. The plaza is the largest shopping mall in Asia, with 200,000 visitors a day, going up to 400,000 on weekends. In Shanghai, the "Get It Louder" show was staged at the Daning Life Hub, which resembles a small-scale city with many outdoor spaces. Other venues were SOHO Shangdu in Beijing, where the exhibits permeated even the underground parking lot, and the Bailian Tianfu Shopping Mall in Chengdu.

Art goes public at the "Get it Louder" show, Daning Life Hub, Shanghai

Ou Ning, one of the founders, says: "Generated by a new series of economic movements, the shopping mall is a spatial form that has thrived in China since [the] 1990s. The act of consumption taking place in this space is also the public life that we are the most familiar with today, and to some extent, it even constitutes a part of our collective memory. The idea behind holding an art exhibition within this kind of large-scale consumerist space, other than being an attempt to break away from the conventional exhibition model of museums and biennials, is particularly in the hope of getting rid of the idea of art as a sanctuary, to enable art to enter people's lives, and to bring it closer to them. Perhaps allowing people to encounter art, to discover it by accident while they are taking part in leisure and consumer activities, is a more effective way to get art into people's hearts than through rigid education."

Other than the main show, "Get It Louder" organizes a series of satellite exhibits and activities called "Homeshows" in small offices and private apartments, comprising installations, lectures, and symposia, which extend the scale and duration of the main event. Ou Ning explains: "An exhibition should be part of daily life, which is easily found everywhere." As a marketing activity, it is very smart. "We build a bridge between designers and sponsors, facilitating their cooperation; thus, transforming design into real productivity. Chivas likes the work of Unmask, which is a Beijing design group. Then, Chivas invited them to design a whiskey glass, cocktail glass, and ice holder. As a result, you could drink Chivas in specially designed glasses by Unmask at the venues of 'Get It Louder' exhibitions. There is another example. Grohe, the sanitary system company from Germany, favors the installation work *Water Corridor* by architect Chen Xudong. Grohe will not only entitle the work, but also plans to include it in its design annual and to invite Chen Xudong to design faucets and other products. Only by being applied in real life, can design reflect its true values."

Groups like "Get It Louder" are seeking and finding a larger role for creativity in contemporary China. Ou Ning says: "In China, these days, everyone is talking about creative industry; even the government is promoting it. However, most people only see the industrial value of creativity, but ignore its social value. 'Get

It Louder '07' places particular emphasis on the social value of creativity. At present, China is still at the stage of a 'post-figurative' society. In other words, the older generations have the power in the society, and the younger generations have little chance to express themselves. Part of the purpose of 'Get It Louder' is to provide the young generation with a channel to release their energy. Consequently, with the average age of the participating artists at around 30, the exhibition also targets young audiences. From a sociological point of view, it helps to meet the psychological needs of young people as an underprivileged social group, and to alleviate latent generational conflicts. This is its social value."

The show addresses social and urban issues in myriad ways. "Moving Soundscape" is a specially curated project that combines sound art and urban geographical research. Numerous Chinese sound artists do research on the peripheral areas of each of the four cities within a distance of a 40-minute car-ride, to sample and analyze each city's architectural styles, functions, and noise index. Each then creates a new sound work based on these data, and installs the work in a car. The audience sits in the car and moves around according to the itinerary defined by the artist. In this way, they can listen to the artist's sound work while at the same time receiving a visual impression of the cityscape. One of the international participants in the show, French architect Benjamin Beller, noticed the great number of available spaces on the back of large billboards in Chinese cities. Through simple design, he turned this space into unsophisticated dwellings, which combine multiple functions: they are still billboards when closed during the day; however, they become kitchens, bedrooms, and balconies when opened up in the evening. As the largest work in "Get It Louder" in 2007, it intends to create and inspire more living spaces for homeless people.

Inspired by the eponymous breakout of 1934, "The Long March" is a multifaceted art and social project that revisits contexts, historic and geographic locations, and challenges the limits of cultural forms through visual display. Its chief curator, Lu Jie, lives in New York. Co-curator Qui Zhijie is one of the bright stars in Beijing's art scene. It is with the symbolic deliverance of the communist ideal to China's proletariat in mind that the new Long Marchers chose to march contemporary art out to China's peripheral populations. Over five months, a curatorial team and two camera crews traveled along the route of the old Long March, documenting the journey and inviting local and international artists to participate by showing their artworks. Each event comprised an exhibition and a forum for debate. En route were encounters with isolated "folk" artists such as Li Tianbing, a photographer who uses an old-fashioned plate camera and makes prints using sunlight, since he has no access to electricity; and Old Jiang, a village painter who has made an extraordinary set of relief portraits of communist leaders in the Wei style of Buddhist sculpture. Like the "Get It Louder" show, but in a completely different environment, "The Long March" takes the discourse of art out into the open, public space.

Creative artists are finding new ways of promoting and selling their work, outside the traditional, elite stranglehold of the galleries. Taiwanese student Wang Yiying's book *Fashion Market*, about London's Spitalfield's and Portobello Road markets, inspired Guangzhou's *City Pictorial* magazine to create the flea market iMart in one of the city's basketball fields. Overcoming the local administration's misgivings about street stalls, some of the brightest young creative people in southern China set up stalls selling sketches, paintings, hand-decorated T-shirts and notebooks, dolls, furniture, cloth shopping bags, CD jackets, and decorative pieces. Hip-hop dancers and rappers added to the fun environment, and business was brisk. iMart has now grown to a bimonthly event, is beginning to attract experienced artists, and has expanded beyond Guangzhou to find a place at the Midi Music Festival in Beijing held in May 2007, and in the New Factories entertainment area in Shanghai during the October holidays later in the year.

In this buzzing environment, from the perspective of the artist, the opportunities to create new work are multiplying in terms of subjects, media, markets, and inspiration. After several decades of a strictly guided, politically enforced, and unidimensional, patriotic artistry, when artists were almost totally cut off from knowing what was happening in the art world outside China, the new-found liberty is being intensively used to fill the gaps and negotiate with the commercial and international art world.

Feng Zhengjie paints huge pink-and-green women's faces, and recently sold one of his works to the Saatchi Gallery in London. An art teacher in Sichuan province before he came to Beijing in 1995, he and his contemporaries stay away from overtly political themes. In his recent work, he borrows the red and green of traditional Chinese New Year paintings, and makes them more acidic as a representation of flashy, modern China. But even as he makes a comment on the changes, he participates in them—for instance, for the sportswear brand adidas, he added the logos of the 2008 Beijing Olympics to the faces of the women he painted.

In the initial stages of China's opening–up era, artists found it difficult to pursue a career devoted to creativity. Their problems stemmed as much from their lack of exposure as from social and family pressures. Oil painter Li Zengguo was born in 1968 in Suzhou, in Jiangsu province, and earned his Bachelor's degree in Art from Jiangsu Normal University. "I liked to paint and draw as a kid but never thought I would be an artist. In the 1980s, as China had just opened up its doors, we were expected to grow up and have a real job and contribute to the party's great mission. So I went to Mining School. But then I realized I'd chosen the wrong profession and went back to school to study art. Then I took a teaching job, got married—it was a happy life. But I gradually realized I needed to devote my time to painting and nothing else. My wife was not very supportive of that. We divorced and I moved to Shanghai to become a full-time painter." It was a decision that he would not regret.

"There are many opportunities here. It is like a train or a tide. You either jump on it and ride it, or you get crushed and buried even if you're on the right track. It makes me push forward constantly. China is becoming more and more open to new ideas and things. Now that people have more money and financial security, they appreciate art more. I no longer feel any pressure to conform. I feel I have the luxury of freedom to express myself in the form that I choose and the subject matter I choose."[6] Li Zengguo has since gone on to exhibit his work in Germany and Canada.

The early 1980s saw some artists begin to address the damage done by the Cultural Revolution, albeit cautiously. The movement was called "Scar Painting" and "Art of the Wounded." By mid-decade, boldly experimental and political works were being created in several parts of China. Art critic Gao Minglu called this explosion of avant-garde art the "'85 Movement," and its aim was nothing less than social and political change. "They felt a very strong responsibility towards social reform," recalled Gao. "This movement was not just for creating an art form or style, rather, the artists' concern was that their activity be a part of the social change."[7] One of the most remarkable pieces to emerge from the '85 Movement was Xu Bing's exquisite art installation, *A Book from the Sky*. Xu is still a leader of Chinese avant-garde art, although he now lives in New York. Xu and many other contemporary artists began to draw on traditional philosophies such as Taoism to create distinctly modern, distinctly Chinese political comment. They also freely mixed traditional methods such as ink painting and scrollwork with Western techniques.

For *A Book from the Sky*, Xu created 4,000 nonsense Chinese written characters, carved them into wood panels in the style of the 11th-century Sung dynasty, and displayed the work on a scroll. It took almost three years of tedious work, from 1987 to 1991, to create. The avant-garde movement quieted after 1989. Some critics think artists also were responding to the public's shift in interest from ideology to money.

Some of the creations of the current generation of artists are ambitious. Between April and September 2007, the Walker Art Center in Minneapolis, in the United States, organized a retrospective of the work of the Chinese artist Huang Yongping, "House of Oracles," at the Vancouver Art Gallery. Forty works, made over the previous 20 years, were on show; they included the cockpit of a US spy plane, a 100-foot-long snake skeleton, and a sculpture of a Beaux Arts-style bank made out of 20,000 kilograms of sand. It is a sculptural environment that is part diorama, part fun house and part menagerie, navigating the East–West divide.

Huang Yongping was born in Xiamen, on the east coast of China. In 1986, inspired by Marcel Duchamp and Dada, he formed the Xiamen Dada Group. Their avant-garde activities are considered to be the first postmodern works in Chinese art. The Paris-based artist has been described by the *New York Times* as "... not one of the crouching tigers of the new Chinese art, but one of its hidden dragons." His exhibition provoked the visitor to re-examine everything from the idea of art, to recent history, to national identity. A three-and-a-half-meter-high, fragile sand sculpture of a British bank alluded to the delicate nature of Western influence on China. A life-size replica of an American spy plane that collided with a Chinese fighter jet—inspired by the event that caused an intense diplomatic row in 2001—was festooned with 300 bats. It raised the questions of media censorship and international news coverage at the time. Even the entrance to the show was designed to provoke. Visitors must pass through a lion's cage, littered with the entrails of a meal consumed some time earlier; it was a metaphor for the artist's own experience as a non-Westerner crossing Western borders.

Some artists are beginning to explore the impact of Western exposure on Chinese culture, as well as the rapid urban development being experienced in China. *Calligraphy Waterfall* is an installation project by the Yangjiang Group, composed of Guogu Zheng, Zaiyan Chen, and Qinglin Sun. It shows a pile of calligraphy paper hardened by wax. Traditional Chinese calligraphers had a high level of scholastic achievement. In contrast, the calligraphic inscriptions on this piece of work are quotations from international news stories, and headlines about terrorism, American politics, and similar themes. The work asks the question: in today's world of information deluge, can traditional Chinese art escape the bombardment of news? In yet another video piece, artist Yang Zhenzhong is seen walking holding the Oriental Pearl TV Tower, the symbol of modern Shanghai, upside down, as he tries to maintain his balance. The work holds up a mirror to people in contemporary China as they struggle to maintain their balance through the profound changes that are under way in China. An installation piece, *Building Dodg'em* by Hao Lu, uses mini-skyscrapers and old Chinese buildings made of acrylic, mounted on toy bulldozers which visitors can move around on a bright pink platform by using a remote control. It suggests that the urban population is at the mercy of the heated, disorderly real estate market in China.[8] These artworks were exhibited at Tokyo's Mori Art Museum between July and September 2005.

At the Inova show titled "Ruins," held in April 2006 at the University of Wisconsin, Milwaukee, in the United States, the same thoughts reappeared in another form. In many of the artworks could be seen mounds of bricks, remnants of the torn-down buildings and homes giving way to progress. With spray-painted, graffiti-like scrawls, Zhang Dali put a face to the marginalized people who had been displaced by such demolitions. He put the shape of a man's profile on to buildings scheduled to be pulled down. In some cases, he knocked out part of the walls in the shape of his signature profile. These profiles stood like witnesses to the change and its human costs. From soon-to-be-gone, rejected structures, Zhang resurrected a sense of the nobility of those lives that are also crumbling and being cast aside. As visually rich as they are conceptually moving, Zhang's photographs of his street art betrayed a sensitive eye for composition as well. Inside the silhouette of his profile shape, he visually layered old and new architecture, shadow and light, flatness and depth, the newly built and the newly deconstructed.[9] These works were telling evidence that Chinese artists were confident about taking the dilemmas of their own society and placing them under international scrutiny.

The new hedonism brought about by the booming economy is proving to be yet another popular subject of exploration by Chinese artists. In 1998, young female painter Yang Fan began to portray the girls in southern Chinese towns. These girls were fashionable, wore heavy makeup, smoked cigarettes, and posed like movie stars. In their urban materialism, they are identical to the young women in Western capitalist countries. Even girls in the countryside prefer international-brand cosmetics, clothes, and other products. Yan's paintings reveal the fantasy of young women in the period of transition: to advance themselves by possessing material goods.

The photographic work of Yang Fudong has a flavor of intellectual conflict. His photography is a simulated play of a scene, reflecting the inward change that the "new professionals" face because of uncertainty about their status, resulting in the transition to being modern, white-collar workers. In 2000, his work entitled *The First Intellectual* showed a white-collar young man, dressed in a bloody and torn suit, standing in the road in Shanghai's finance and trade district, and attempting to fight with bricks in his hands. Yang Fudong's work tries to express the internal injury that intellectuals have suffered following China's acceptance of capitalism.

The Jelly Generation artists were born in the 1980s. Swept along by the tide of modernity engulfing the mainland, they have been described as a generation that is a bundle of contradictions— both free-spirited and lonely, open-minded and self-centered. Zhang Qing, who curated their exhibition at the Shanghai Art Museum in May–June 2007, says, "Their minds are both pure and blank. Like jelly, they are the product of their time and live in an infant-like world." These artists, quite metaphorically, pour their thoughts and ideas into any medium that can contain them successfully. Illustrator Yan Wei's black-and-white illustrations seem as if they have been torn from the pages of a book of fairytales: little girls are stranded in pools of ink; armies of birdhouses sprout legs and wander into the distance. An *Alice in Wonderland* world, it is more about worry than wonder. Explaining her work, she says: "We look back at the time when we were young and feel a sense of loss." Chen Yun portrays a life full of leisure and affluence. Her computer-generated illustrations are surreal, with fish, flowers, and legs floating in a burgundy vortex. The flowers represent the impermanence of both love and beauty; the fish symbolize the sexual. She explains, "I was exploring the issue of freedom; water is the fish's habitat and at the same time, it provides freedom." She calls her work "Fantasy Reality," challenging the limits established during her childhood and reveling in her newfound artistic freedom. Bu Hua works in Flash® animation, using playfulness, dense colors, and black lines to describe her generation in an abstract manner. Her work *Youth is Harmful to Health* suggests that adolescence is a double-edged sword. "My work is all very *suiyi*," she says—random and free. The Jelly Generation has embraced the randomness of life itself, and by doing so, has found new forms of creative expression.[10]

While many artists have already made a name in the international art market and among museums, there are thousands queuing up. The Artists' Village Gallery, one of the largest galleries in Beijing at more than 4,000 square meters, is located in Songzhuang in the capital's eastern suburbs. There are more than 500 contemporary

Chinese artists living in villages around Songzhuang, each hoping to break on to the national and international stage. Sally Liu, who owns the gallery with her husband, says: "Of course we are trying to make money, but at the same time we want to give back to the community by helping Chinese artists promote their work, especially the ones living around us."

Wei Ding, executive director of the Songzhuang Art Center, commented: "The aim of the Artists' Village, and more specifically this Center, is to provide a platform for communication between Chinese and international artists. To sustain and promote China's flourishing contemporary art scene, we need to foster more exchange between East and West."

Technology is beginning to play a key role in the way Chinese contemporary art is presented and promoted. London's renowned Saatchi Gallery announced in May 2007 that it is launching a new, non-profit website in Chinese to allow artists in China the opportunity to present their work to a global audience. "Your Gallery in Mandarin" will be part of the overall Saatchi Gallery site, which is the largest interactive art gallery site in the world with over four million hits a day. In addition to free postings and translations, the Chinese site will host an interactive blog, forum, and chat room.

The decision to create the "Your Gallery in Mandarin" website was made after it became apparent that Chinese students were already putting their profiles on the general Saatchi Gallery site, despite the fact that they spoke little or no English. "We began noticing that Chinese artists were posting their work and seemed really keen to show their art and communicate with other students and artists. The language barrier was obviously a problem, though," says Kieran McCann, head of creative development for the site.

Yang Fudong is an artist who uses technology to explore the conflict between opposing forces. A partner in Nokia's "Connect to Art" project, and having worked with Siemens previously, he believes that collaboration between the corporate and the art worlds can be beneficial, as long as both work toward the same goal. Yang believes that one of the goals for an artist should be to find new vehicles for experiencing and sharing art. That's where technology comes in. Yang hopes that the Nokia project will encourage the development of a new medium, one that would allow art lovers to download works through their cell phones and thereby open up art ownership to a greater audience. It's happening with music on a large scale, so why not with art?

Art in China is constantly making transitions, and the phases in art history are indicative of the sentiment and values of the people and the polity. The Peasant Painting Movement is one such manifestation of the role of art evolving from political propaganda to postmodern kitsch. In the 1950s, farmers from Huxian county, in Shaanxi province, began painting pictures as they were engaged in the physical activity of building a reservoir. These paintings were made to record their work, as well as to inspire themselves to work better. Without access to proper materials, they used natural materials such as lime, soot, and the red soil of the area in the classic folk tradition. The county Communist Party authorities noticed their work and brought in professional artists who could teach the workers to paint. "People need art, and art needs more people" was coined as a new slogan. It was a new understanding of art being practiced by common people instead of the intelligentsia or the bourgeoisie. As the painters interacted with the party, the themes began to be tinged with the propaganda of the farmers' vision of a communist paradise—good crops, stables filled with healthy cattle, happy kite-flying children, sufficient food, and fun at the local festivities. The painters interpreted even a normally tedious task as a celebration of life. A scene of harvesting corn got a cheerful touch of butterflies and colorful dress worn by the farmers; a fishing scene was brightened up with a gaily painted boat, an arched bridge, and lotuses floating on the water. With titles such as *I Grow Grain and Cotton for our Motherland* and *Never Forget the State after a Good Harvest*, these became the favorite showpieces for national party leaders to prove to the outside world that ordinary people, given a happy living environment, could produce art.

The painting movement in Jinshan village, an hour's drive from Shanghai, began on a different note. In the early 1970s, some painters from Shanghai visited the village and noticed that the local women were skilled at embroidery and weaving. They also painted frescoes on the walls above their kitchen stoves. One of the

Artist at work, Jinshan Peasant Painting Village

painters, Wu Tongzhuang, took the women to the Shanghai Art
School where he began teaching them how to paint the same designs
using paper and watercolor. In January 1977, the painters held their
first exhibition at the Shanghai Art Museum and shot to instant fame.
As they painted the rustic scenes, the use of bright colors and the
depiction of objects and people in a playful manner gave the paintings
a childlike feel. "Jinshan farmer painting is somewhat similar to
children's drawing, relying on imagination instead of professional
skill," says Chen Xiu, who belongs to a family that has produced
three generations of painters. Her father, Chen Fulin's work has
been exhibited at the British Museum. The local government saw
this as an opportunity to boost the local economy, through both
the paintings and tourism. They encouraged giving the paintings as
diplomatic gifts, boosting their popularity overseas. They formed
the Jinshan Peasant Painting Academy in 1989, and enlisted more
than 100 peasant painters. A fund worth RMB10 million (US$1.3
million) was set up to look after, train, and promote the artists.
In 2006, they brought several artists together and created a living
museum and painting space, where visitors could watch the artists

at work as well as buy their paintings—at source. The option of buying the paintings online, of course, does exist. Aided by a multimedia campaign, with elements of public relations, word-of-mouth, celebrity endorsement, e-commerce, and event management, Jinshan painting has been built as a brand.

Farmer's home, Jinshan Peasant Painting Village

Art galleries on Moganshan Lu, Shanghai

Creativity is now beginning to influence the use of living and working spaces in China. Increasingly, mirroring the development of art districts in the West such as London's Chelsea and New York's Soho, artists and other creative folks are coming to roost in what was once dilapidated urban quarters. Shanghai's Moganshan Lu was once a small lane abutting Suzhou Creek, filled with dilapidated warehouses and factories earmarked for demolition. In the late 1990s, artists, sculptors, and photographers discovered that the empty, spacious halls were suitable as studio spaces, and began to move in. It was only a matter of time before the local authorities recognized the area's potential and canceled the demolition. Emboldened by the move, and as their work began to fetch them higher prices, the creative community ingeniously started to renovate the spaces, even as they preserved the original architecture. The creative community quickly found their cause supported by art dealers, gallery owners, curators, coffeehouse operators, and club managers. Today, there is an unmistakable buzz to the place. Most of the warehouses have been refurbished. Shiny new cars fill the parking lot, many owned by the artists themselves, others by prosperous art dealers. Tour buses disgorge school students and

Visitors at the Shanghai Biennale

foreign tourists. Live music performances fill up the loungy restaurants, and sometimes the art galleries in the evenings. Shanghai's biggest art businesses— Eastlink Gallery, BizArt, ArtScene, M50, Shanghart—all operate out of this place. *The Economist* touts it as the place to go "if you're looking for investment."

Dashanzi Art District in Beijing's northwest quarter is no different. The walled compound of red-brick factories, warehouses, and offices set on a tree-lined grid of streets and lanes offers a miniature sanctuary from the urban sprawl. This former munitions factory space was designed in the 1950s by East German architects, who adopted a Bauhaus-style design. In around 2000, the lofty interior spaces and homogenous lighting conditions seemed perfect for a group of artists wishing to resettle here. As a culturally historic piece amidst a modern landscape, the structure of factories plays a key role in keeping the Dashanzi Art District alive. The architectural quality inherent in the structures—angled windows, high ceilings, and large windows—makes the contemporary art displayed even more surprising and enjoyable than if it were housed in a conventional gallery or museum. For Chinese artists reinterpreting communist propaganda, particularly the images and figures of Chairman Mao, Dashanzi contains remnants of that history itself. Fading slogans exhorting the toiling masses can still be seen on some of the factories' walls, reminding artists and visitors of the fervor that fueled the Chinese Cultural Revolution. It is a different matter that graffiti is emblazoned on the same walls today, some with Nike swooshes embedded among the stylized imagery of contemporary China. Since 2000, around 300 businesses have been set up here—painting, sculpture, photography

Graffiti at 798 Art District, Beijing

Various installations at 798 Art District, Beijing

studios, fashion stores, art bookstores, music shops, publishing and consulting companies, advertising agencies, interior design and architecture firms, handicraft and pottery studios, restaurants, and bars. While not all are strictly creative businesses, they all thrive in the "creative atmosphere" that the Dashanzi Art District has come to represent. Companies such as Motorola, Sony, Ford, and Omega are beginning to launch their new brands in this environment, hoping to gain from the assemblage of creative minds.

Even as the nouveau-riche property developers across China emerge as prime buyers, some real estate developers have found art and innovative design an effective marketing tool for building a high-brow image among consumers and society at large. They reckon that if the spaces that home-buyers occupy are filled with artworks, there will be a disproportionate increase in their value, in addition to this being a unique selling proposition. Examples of successful cases include the Shanghe Art Gallery in Chengdu, and Modern Town, Jindian Garden, Yuanyang Center, and Huarun Land in Beijing.

In the 1990s, real estate developer Pan Shiyi envisaged that his properties would be different from the steel and blue glass-encased behemoths that were sprouting up all over Beijing. He wanted to paint the outside of his proposed apartment complex in bright primary colors. No way, said his critics then; China isn't colorful. The government had recently underlined that point by regulating that all public buildings should be painted gray. But Pan, who grew up in Gansu province (gray, gray, and more gray), was convinced that China's history didn't necessarily condemn its citizens to a monochromatic life. After all, he remembered, the Xi'an terracotta warriors, now a muddy shade of gray, were originally painted with such breathtaking colors that some of the dyers were reputedly killed lest they give away the secret to the brilliant tints. So, Pan and his wife Zhang Xin ignored the skeptics and built the daring Soho New Town, a multihued complex of apartments and offices in eastern Beijing.[11] They went ahead and commissioned works to be displayed in these properties. *Slides*, by Wang Xingwei, shows a group of businessmen wearing suits and ties, who, instead of taking the elevator to work, take the colorful playground slides used by children. Ai Weiwei's *Jacks* brings a childhood game back to life. He tries to make people see things from a different angle from his *Tilted House*. The small slanting house follows the same design as Soho New Town's buildings, leading the viewer to wonder: which is tilted and which is straight?

As art creates financial value—the rentals at Dashanzi have increased tenfold since 2000—it remains to be seen if that becomes a barrier to new artists entering the scene and injecting fresh blood; or if the injection of money would be a stimulant. Critics of Dashanzi and Moganshan Lu have said that, unlike the "Get It Louder" shows, these galleries are targeted at foreigners. After all, juxtapositions of Chairman Mao with Mickey Mouse probably don't have as much appeal among the Chinese population as among foreigners.

That criticism notwithstanding, the moot point remains that aesthetic appreciation is beginning to permeate almost every corner of Chinese society. The very ubiquity of artworks, at a huge range of price points, makes it easy for both the common person and the elite to inject beauty—Chen Yifei's mission—into their lives.

---

[1] "China's Red Hot Art Market," *BusinessWeek*, July 17, 2007.

[2] John Ruwitch, "Chinese Artists Capitalize on Avant-garde Boom," http://shanghaichase.blogspot.com/2007/06/Chinese-artists-capitalise-on-avant.html.

[3] Martin Paetsch, "China's Art Factories—Van Gogh from the Sweatshop," *Der Spiegel*, August 23, 2006.

[4] www.time.com/time/asia/features/china_cul_rev/stylist.html.

[5] Ou Ning, "Everyone is a Curator," www.getitlouder.com.

[6] Interview with Li Zengguo: www.mandarinfineart.com/director_oct05.htm.

[7] www.cnn.com/SPECIALS/1999/china.50/inside.china/art.overview/.

[8] Cao Yin, "Follow Me! Chinese Art at the Threshold of the New Millennium," www.studio-international.co.uk/reports/chinese_evolution.asp.

[9] Mary Louise Schumacher, "Revolution Simmers below China's Sleek Evolution," *Milwaukee Journal Sentinel*, April 14, 2006.

[10] Rebecca Catching, "Rubber Soul—The Jelly Generation Comes of Age," *That's Shanghai*, July 2007.

[11] Hannah Beech, "The Bright House,"–www.time.com/time/asia/features/china_cul_rev/developer.html.

Showbiz and Shooting Stars
Finding an outlet for creative talent on or behind the screen

"It's not that I wanted to be an actor, it's that I didn't want to be a dancer! I was trained in traditional Chinese dance, and after working so hard it seemed unfair to just disappear into a group."

Zhang Ziyi, actress

Memories of old Hollywood, at Songjiang Film City

On July 8, 2007, Beijing TV aired a story called "Transparency" on its lifestyle channel. In the story, a reporter, armed with a hidden camera, showed how a dim-sum booth owner used cardboard pulp as a pork substitute, softened it with an industrial chemical, added pork flavoring, and then sold it to unsuspecting customers. Under attack on food and drug safety issues, the Chinese government wanted to show that it had increased its surveillance, and the program showed that there were indeed investigative journalists on the prowl. As soon as the story went on air, quite expectedly, the international media picked it up. From Fox News to the BBC to the *International Herald Tribune*, the contamination story began fanning insecurities about Chinese food imports. "China Cuts Corners," screamed ABC News. Beijing's food safety watchdog and the Industrial and Commercial Administration swung into action, launching a city-wide inspection of every dim-sum booth. They found nothing. Had it all been covered up so quickly?

It was then that the truth emerged—a remarkable story of journalistic inventiveness. After some local people had complained about finding some paper in pork buns, freelance reporter Zi Beijia was asked by his editors to cover the story. For 10 days, Beijia went around, buying buns at different roadside dim-sum booths, but could find nothing wrong with them. When time was running out, he decided to concoct a story. He inveigled the owner of a dim-sum booth to prepare the dim sums stuffed with cardboard, as he filmed the story. To make it sound authentic, he interviewed one of the men at the booth. For a couple of days, Zi Beijia's attempt to garner higher TV ratings succeeded. When the subterfuge was discovered, however, the action was swift. He was arrested, the deputy director of the channel and its producer were fired, and the editor-in-chief of the TV station received an administrative punishment. There were a lot of red faces everywhere.

Driven by an insatiable thirst to get their 15 minutes of fame, thousands of ordinary people in China are looking for every possible opportunity to be heroes. Like the young Zhang Ziyi felt, just being a dancer among many isn't enough for them. They must be recognized as individuals; as being the best. The desire for stardom is fiercely competitive, and it is here that we are witnessing a flowering of creative talent.

The wildly popular reality musical talent shows *My Hero* and *Super Girl* epitomize this sense of competitiveness in contemporary China. Until 2005, Chinese viewers were fed with a one-way stream of entertainment, most recently characterized by the romantic soap opera from South Korea, *Winter Sonata*. Then, for a few months that year eight million mostly young Chinese decided to vote.

Sponsored by Mengnniu Dairy, *Super Girl*, a talent hunt show that rewarded contestants for their singing and stage presence, inspired unashamedly by *American Idol*, took the airwaves by storm. *Super Girl* was China's first nationally televised show of its kind, according to Liao Ke, its co-creator and a program designer for state-owned Hunan province satellite television. He says that the program grew out of China's rising standard of living, which spawned more "colorful" entertainment options than in the days when art and entertainment were required to serve the country's communist revolution. "Everybody wants to express themselves, and Hunan TV just became the platform," he says. "It's like our logo says: 'If you want to sing, sing.'"

Hunan TV's exhortations encouraged some 120,000 girls and women to take part in the contest. To reach the Chengdu auditions, one teenager endured a 15-hour train trip from her home in western China, according to the weekly magazine *Liaowang Dongfan Zhoukan*. One woman from Fujian province reportedly traveled to each city in turn, losing in the first round every time. She spent more than three months' wages before finally abandoning her quest for fame. Through a series of provincial contests, the number of performers was whittled down—and those on the shortlist became increasingly stylized as the show progressed. The show catapulted China's young women into a *Super Girl* rebellion, in which traits such as assertiveness, confidence, and creative eccentricity made a thrilling triumph over the old, introverted ideal of pretty-girl Chinese pop.

The finals, held on August 30, 2005, were watched by 400 million people. After the frenetic voting was over, Li Yuchun, a music student whose tomboy looks, spiky hair, and onstage confidence were already the talk of Chinese chat rooms, won with 3.5 million votes. With several brand endorsements secured, she multiplied her earnings to far greater levels than the US$6,000 prize money. Before the end of the year, she had made it on to the cover of *Time* magazine. Coca-Cola, Crest toothpaste, Swatch, Amoi mobile phones, ShenZhou computer, TiaoTiaoLong candy, and Yi-Chun down coat signed her on as brand endorser. (Even third-placed Zhang Liangying landed a host of endorsement contracts: TCL laptop, JinMaiLang tea drink, and Honda Civic cars, for which she sang the jingle accompanying the TV commercial.) Shopping malls across China were stocked with Li Yuchun mugs, T-shirts, and key-rings. The government even issued a stamp in her honor. The Chinese Academy of Social Science estimated that the 2005 *Super Girl* contest raked in about RMB766 million (US$95.75 million).

The *Super Girl* phenomenon gave rise to a socio-political discussion. Li Yuchun sings aggressively: loud songs, and songs written for men. "It's contrary to orthodox singing and traditional aesthetics," said Cai Lin, associate professor of sociology and gender studies at Tongji University, explaining how a tomboy became one of China's most important social figures overnight. "The most popular girls these days are not meek or ladylike. As society opens up, women can be brave, more independent and outgoing like boys." Commenting on the achievement orientation that *Super Girl* underlined, Chen Shangjun, professor of humanities and literature at Fudan University, added: "In every sphere of Chinese life—social, economic and academic—it's simply too difficult for young people to beat everyone and win. There are so many restrictions and you have to be perfect and extremely lucky to attract any attention at all."[1]

It was entirely another matter that the success of the program had the authorities in Beijing slightly worried about the precedent it may set for more unregulated forms of pop culture, but even more so about unleashing the power of the youth vote.

In the following year, 2006, Shanghai Dragon TV's *My Hero* replaced *Super Girl* as China's most-watched reality TV show. The show's motto—"How many roads must a man walk down before they call him a man"—taken from the Bob Dylan song "Blowing in the Wind," was a hit with viewers. The TV ad for the program said, "*My Hero* shows how frogs can become princes." The main competition took place in six major cities, including Shanghai, Beijing, Hangzhou, Chengdu, Chongqing, and Dalian. The handsome contestants sang, danced, and even performed push-ups to impress the judges. Then came a question-and-answer session. "Why do you think you are a good man?" or "What would you do if someone says your girlfriend isn't pretty?" Their female fans hung on their every word.

Readers of a mass-selling lifestyle and entertainment magazine published in Guangzhou started a bidding frenzy for the male contestants. The postings read: "50 yuan for inviting Xiang Ding to dinner"; "500 yuan for a date with the handsome Tibetan contestant Pubagya [Pu Bajia]." The postings created protests from the contestants, but they reflected the craze for the all-male show. Zheng Zueling, a junior middle–school student from Jiaxing in Zhejiang province, spent several hundred renminbi on sending text messages to vote for her favorite star. "I almost ran out of pocket money," she said. "However, it was a happy experience. We share a dream of stardom but the contestant is brave enough to actually do it."[2] "The women's era has come and gone. Now it is the time to enjoy the charms of the men," wrote the popular Taiwan singer and TV actress Yi Nengjing in her blog. She was one of the *My Hero* judges.

My Hero's ratings in Shanghai reached 5.3%, while *Super Girl* slipped to 0.2%, according to the AC Nielsen Company. *My Hero* relies on a simple format, according to entertainment journalist Guo Gang. "It is simply amateurs providing the entertainment and has-beens dominating the panels of judges who rule on who stays and who is jettisoned into the horrific void of anonymity," he said. The overall champion won RMB300,000 (US$37,500) for business development plus a brand-new Mazda Familla sedan car. There were other awards, such as "Best Teamwork Spirit," "Best Body," and "Best Ability." Pu Bajia, Wu Jianfei, and Song Xiaobo, the final three contestants, walked away with much adulation and many brand endorsements. Bajia was signed on for AMing Food, Bright XinShuang yoghurt, and Qinghai–Tibet Railway. Wu Jianfei endorses Lycra, which sponsored the show, and men's cosmetics brand Tayoi. The 2007 winner was Jing Boran, an 18-year-old from Shenyang in China's northeast. Jing wasn't even one of the wannabe stars. One of the show's directors spotted him at a Shenyang restaurant where he was dining with friends, and urged him to enter the contest. When he arrived in Shanghai to participate, it was the first time he had ventured out of his hometown.

The "packaging" and gender neutrality of the winners of *Super Girl* and *My Hero* is spurring social commentators to question the very values that Chinese society, especially the youth, has come to embrace. Wang Yong is an acerbic critic. He writes:

> Since when have tomboys and sissy girls become in vogue I have no idea. But major TV stations have vied with each other since 2005 to produce "top singers" who sing poorly but look and act like the opposite sex. Most have won music awards, not the least for their "artistic talent" but simply for their strange looks and outlook. Ugly is no longer as ugly does, under the false light of the stage. The ugliest have become the most welcome to an uninformed audience, thanks to the manipulation of those TV stations that prefer strange personality to professionalism.[3]

Wang then attempts to reinstate some sanity and true music appreciation into the audience. He writes of one of the contestants in Hunan TV's show *Happy Boys*:

> [Chen Chusheng] is a man of 26 years, quiet looking, apparently unswayed by waves of emotion. His eyes are deep and appear to gaze far into the distance. He smiles, but only mildly. He looks a bit shy, but is quite manly, having weathered the vicissitudes of life since he had to work at age 19. His love songs are mainly about the hardship and coldness in city life and a strong mind in the face of setbacks … I thank Hunan TV, which allows fans a big say in deciding winners. I salute Hunan TV for having presented us a true man, a true musician, a true idol of our times.

Entertainment reality shows are a telling symptom of the sweeping change that is engulfing the entertainment and media business in China. This change is being spurred on by a combination of economic and creative forces. There are now 3,000 different stations beaming shows across the country's airwaves, and the pressure to come up with appealing content is huge. Reality TV offers a distinct advantage in grabbing those eyeballs, and the inspiration for such shows is often Western. A version of Donald Trump's *Apprentice* series is in the pipeline, but with a distinctly Chinese spin, particularly the title, *Wise Man Takes All.* Zhejiang TV's reality show *True Boys Dreaming of Olympics* features Olympic diving gold medalist Tian Liang. The former athlete acts as the chief coach for 24 boys from all over China, who form two teams and compete against each other in 28 events that mimic the events at the Beijing Olympics.

All this is quite a far cry from the early days of Chinese television. The transformation from the state-controlled single station broadcasting political propaganda to a market- and viewer-led plentitude is a remarkable testament to the unleashing of creative forces in China.

Television broadcasting began in China at seven o'clock on the evening on May 1, 1958, during the era of the Great Leap Forward. The first TV drama, a 30-minute play entitled *A Veggie Cake* (*Yikou Cai Bingzi*), directed by Hu Xu, was aired soon after, on June 15. At the time, for Hu Xu and other television professionals, the birth of Chinese TV drama wasn't an act of imitating the foreign, but an indigenous phenomenon. Between 1958 and 1966, nearly 200 TV dramas were produced—all performed and telecast live (in what became known as the "*zhibo qi* period"). The production of these dramas was an integral part of the nation-building campaign, and all TV producers joined hands with teachers and propagandists to become "engineers of the soul." TV drama production came to a halt during the Cultural Revolution. When it resumed in 1978, Chinese TV stations began broadcasting a mix of foreign shows and indigenous dramas. Foreign dramas played a key role in filling up the time slots. After years of being isolated from the world, viewers began to see the West through programs such as *Remington Steele*, *Falcon Crest*, *Hunter*, and *Man from Atlantis*. (It is believed that *Dynasty* was a favorite of Deng Xiaoping.) The Japanese soap opera *Oshin* became very popular. In 1978, the 32 TV stations at the time produced a meager eight TV dramas. Indigenous dramas, such as *New Star* (*Xin Xing*), began taking on topical issues such as social and economic reform. Up until the 1980s, television was a propaganda product whose main role was to disseminate positive role models to society.

In the late 1980s, and into the 1990s, the growth in the Chinese television industry was unprecedented. In 1987, there were 366 stations producing 1,500 dramas.[4] As the output proliferated, critics and scholars began creating sub-genres: *lianxu ju* (television serial), *tongsu ju* (popular drama), *qingjie ju* or *yanqing ju* (melodrama), *shinei ju* (indoor drama), *feizao ju* (soap opera), *xiju* (comedy), *qingjing xiju* (sitcom), *lishi ju* (historical drama), *wuxia ju* (martial arts drama), and *jingfei ju* (detective and crime drama). Michael Keane refers to this period as the "market era," characterized by "outbreaks of autonomy."[5]

Yearnings (*Kewang*, 50 episodes, 1990) and *Beijingers in New York* (*Bejingren zai Niuyue*, 21 episodes, 1993) marked the maturity of the "soap opera" as a full-blown Chinese genre. Directed by Zheng Xiaolong and broadcast by Beijing TV and CCTV, *Yearnings* told the story of two families intertwined by circumstances. Similar to in America, where the term "soap opera" took root because of the detergent and soap advertisements that appeared during the broadcast, every episode of *Yearnings* began with a TV commercial for the detergent brand *Dailaoli* ("Save Your Labor"). Commercials were built into the TV subtext quite early in China. *Beijingers in New York* marked the beginning of the genre that explored the changing gender and power equations that were emerging in the new China, as a result of the exposure to Western cultures and people. Shot entirely in New York, it portrayed the life of Jiang Wen, a Chinese artist who emigrates to New York, his wife Guo Yan, mistress Ah Chun, daughter Ning Ning, and business competitor David McCarthy. In the narrative, the Chinese man competes with the white male for both women and capital—his wife leaves him for McCarthy, but he eventually takes over McCarthy's factory. The ideology represented in the serial is one of an aggressive, confident Chinese male who can take on Westerners on their home turf. This is depicted in scenes such as one where Jiang Wen is being entertained by a white prostitute, as much as in scenes showing his business battles with McCarthy. TV serials like this one, and the later *Russian Girls in Harbin* (*Eluosi Gunian zai Harbin*, 1994) and *Foreign Babes in Beijing* (*Yangniu zai Beijing*, 1996), fascinate the audience because of their attempt to define the Chinese identity in the global cultural imagination. The manner in which Chinese men are able to conquer foreign women is as much a potent representation of the resurrection of Chinese masculinity as a victory of the Chinese nation itself.[6]

Stories of the Editorial Office (*Bianjibu de Gushi*, 25 episodes, 1991) was regarded as the birth of the Chinese-style situation comedy. The serial is a black comedy about a magazine editorial team coming to grips with the commercial market; it satirizes tabloid journalism and how the pursuit of advertising revenue sometimes undermines journalistic integrity. The iconoclastic urban dramas of the early 1990s generated immense creative energy in the TV market in China and were followed by a host of imitations. By 1993, the success of such serials was creating concerns about public morality, and the government began reining in artistic freedom. During the latter part of the 1990s, producers took the safe path of avoiding content that could be construed as morally decadent.

Until *Sex and the City* and *Desperate Housewives*. Though not broadcast on TV channels, the serials—available in the form of pirated DVDs—are widely watched in urban China. Taking inspiration from *Sex and the City* and the Taiwanese cartoon serial *Hot Ladies* (*Se Nulang*), the serial *Pink Ladies* (*Fenhong Nulang*) was born. Depicting the romantic adventures of four unmarried women, the serial used four caricatures of a pretty woman, a traditional woman, a feminist, and a happy-go-lucky woman to explore courtship, romance, marriage, and life as a single woman. *Feels Like Falling in Love* (*Haoxiang Haoxiang Tan Lianai*) features actress Jiang Wenli and pop star Na Ying, and shows four women, all successful in their careers, financially independent, and socially popular, struggling in their romantic relationships. Once more, these "pink dramas" (so called because of their high female viewership) are indicative of the fascination with romance and divorce; while also suggesting that the hold of the state's censors has eased. Viewers of these programs find that the situations presented are dramatic representations of their own reality.

Overlapping with the popularity of these new Chinese TV dramas and the exposure to new Western entertainment is the "Korean wave." In 2004, *Winter Sonata* became a huge hit in China. It tells the intertwined stories of a girl from Chuncheon named Jung Yujin, her childhood friend, Kim Sang Hyuk, and the dark and mysterious Kang Joon Sang, a transfer student from Seoul. The complex saga encompasses family feuds, car accidents, bouts of amnesia, the dark pasts of parents, misunderstandings, and mistaken identity. The star-crossed lovers are united in a finale that elicited bucketloads of tears from the serial's adoring fans. Besides the gripping story, many viewers simply fell in love with its handsome hero, Kim Sang Hyuk, played by Park Yong Ha, and with the locale, Namiseom Island, which has since become a favorite tourist attraction for Chinese visiting South Korea. Another extremely popular serial is *Jewel in the Palace* (*Dae Jang Geum*), which is based on the true story of Jang Geum, a Korean girl living at the time of the Chosun dynasty, whose parents were killed for political reasons. Through her intelligence, resourcefulness, goodness, sweetness, and selflessness, she becomes one of the most talented cooks in the Korean palace. When she is later framed and loses her position, rather than accept defeat and exile, she fights her way back. She eventually becomes the king's personal doctor, a feat unheard of for a woman during those times. What makes the show different from the average costume drama is the prominent role played by food. At the beginning, Jang Geum is a kitchen maid in the palace, and much of the drama centers around how the cooks prepare food for the emperor, create new types of cuisine, and compete with each other to win the hearts, minds, and stomachs of their superiors. Court intrigue, plots and conspiracies, heart-rending romance, and a cooking show all in one!

These dramas, focusing on inter-family intrigue, respect for parents, overcoming hardships, and so on, found their primary audience among older viewers. What the older Chinese found appealing was the adherence in Korea to essential and traditional values, which China has abandoned in its quest for modernization. Korean dramas offered readily identifiable themes of family, hardship, intrigue, and sacrifice, all set against the backdrop of a society driven by Confucian values that were very similar to traditional Chinese ones. Some households actually claimed that watching these television serials improved their family relations. While watching, they fought less, and the shows provided something to talk about.

The historical drama genre, which is populated by representations of China's imperial history, is another key area where viewers are being reminded of China's traditional Confucian values. *Yongzheng Dynasty* (1999), *Kangxi Dynasty* (2001), and *Qianlong Dynasty* (2003), among others, featured the emperors and patriots who struggled against internal corruption and social injustice as well as external threats, feeding the public's fantasy for a time of heroic figures and events. Mesmerized by the palace politics and nostalgic for an era of just rule that never was, the Chinese public genuinely welcomed such dramas, delighting in their contemporary relevance. Subjects and themes that would invite censorship in contemporary settings—government corruption, political infighting and power struggles, moral cynicism, public unrest, and so on—get prime-time airing in revisionist Qing dramas.

The 44-episode prime-time blockbuster *Yongzheng Dynasty* featured one of the most controversial Qing dynasty emperors, Yongzheng. In portraying a moralistic emperor who forcefully fends off his political opponents, attacks corruption, and fights to protect ordinary people, the show covertly insinuates a critical commentary on the state of affairs in contemporary Chinese society and politics. Yongzheng is deftly made to epitomize integrity and inner strength in a leader. In an era of rampant political corruption and moral cynicism, Yongzheng naturally appealed to Chinese audiences. To some, Yongzheng was suggestive of former Chinese premier Zhu Rongji, whose efforts to curb government corruption have earned him a reputation as a contemporary graft-buster.

The revival of Confucian values as the solution to the Chinese state's current lack of guiding ideology is not universally endorsed by China's intellectuals and policy-makers. Professor Hu Xingdou, a political scientist at the Beijing Institute of Technology, considers Confucius's doctrine of suppressing one's desires and adhering to a high level of moral etiquette unrealistic in a modern society built upon material gain. He advocates adherence to more tangible systems of accountability, such as Western concepts of individual human rights and freedoms, democratic government, and the rule of law. Yet, Confucius's notion of a self-sacrificing ruler dovetails neatly with China as a one-party state. Since coming to power in 2004, Hu Jintao's administration has often alluded to the Confucian precept of officials "dedicating themselves to the interests of the public."[7]

The multiplicity of genres, the rapid evolution in the last 25 years, and the quick adaptation to a changing political and social sensitivity is clearly indicative of the creative ferment in the Chinese television industry. I would argue that the industry has taken greater risks and has pushed creative barriers to a greater extent than has the marketing communications industry, certainly in the area of television advertising. Bound by regulation and its own preoccupation with aiming for the "belly of the market," it has assumed a level of social and cultural conservativeness that is greater than the reality. To take one example, it is now common for young Chinese to cohabit before marriage. However, you would not find a single TV commercial that explicitly shows unmarried couples living together in the same home. If there are depictions of young romance, it is outside the home—in restaurants, bars, shopping malls, and during picnics. Soap operas don't propagate such morality, and are constantly testing the limits.

At the same time, the entertainment reality shows are challenging gender stereotypes. Once again, this is an area that the TV commercials veer away from; they find it convenient to reinforce the stereotype of the dominant male, the sex-siren, and the venerable, wise old man or woman. The effeminate male and the dominatrix woman are often stylized characters who may add a comic or dramatic element to the storyline, but rarely are they the heroes. Where the commercial messages do hit home is when they are whipping up the hysteria over newly created stars, or creating the demand for stardom. It is a promise that is hard to beat in a fame-seeking populace.

China's film industry earned US$337 million at the box office in 2006, up from US$80 million the previous year. It was a big leg-up for the industry. A total of 330 domestic feature films were produced in 2006, but only 110 played in cinemas. Eighty-

Filming in progress at Songjiang Film City

two new theaters were constructed in that year, taking the total number in China to only 1,325, with 3,034 screens—which is about one screen for every 428,477 people. The paucity of screens means there is intense competition for theatrical release. Independent and small budget films never end up on the big screen.

The state of China's film industry, both content-wise and commercially, is shaped by what is happening culturally and politically in China and the world. People in China are currently in the throes of a moral, historical, and existential crisis. The 5,000-year-old cultural continuity that determined society's ethical underpinnings and identity was shattered by 10 years of turmoil. Into the vacuum left behind by the Cultural Revolution, the capitalist world's methods and values were hungrily devoured, faster than they could be digested and assimilated. This supercharged cultural context puts enormous pressure on the role of cinema, as art and as entertainment. Traditionally, cinema in China had had a nationalistic or reflective role. In the newly capitalized marketplace, it is increasingly shaped by the exigencies of investment and profit; in the global sphere, it seeks and has to compete for recognition, in the same way that companies, athletes, and other creative artists need to.

Cinema was introduced into China, very soon after its invention in 1896, by French, American, and Spanish showmen. These early entrepreneurs rented venues such as theaters, restaurants, and teahouses, where they showed short movies either as interludes to the running operas, or during Chinese variety shows. The first film made in China, *Conquering Dingjun Shan* (1905), was based on an existing Peking opera and was performed by a leading opera actor, which ensured the film's popularity. It wasn't until 1908 that a cinema exclusively for film exhibition was built in Shanghai by the Spaniard Antonio Ramos. Ramos would go on to build a chain of theaters in the city. The first serious attempt at filmmaking was by Zhang Sichuan and Zheng Zhenqiu, who made *The Difficult Couple*, a comical short film that satirized elaborate Chinese wedding rituals. The early films projected ethnic culture as a spectacle. In the 1920s, filmmaking was a speculative business. Small companies made one film, raked in the profits, and then closed shop. In this environment, Zhang and Zheng formed the Mingxing (Star) Company and began to specialize in family dramas, telling stories about life in a changing society where

Confucian values such as filial piety and female chastity were glorified. This cinema was steeped in traditionalism, quite opposed to the radicals of the May Fourth Movement of the time. Zheng had decided that his cinema would be about moral education through popular entertainment.

At the same time, the Shao brothers founded their Tianyi (Unique) Company in 1925, but chose to adapt for the big screen Chinese folktales and legends that were already popular. The brothers invested in building a theater chain, and this combination of production and distribution model resulted in their film *White Snake* becoming enormously successful in 1926. Mingxing Company responded by producing an 18-part martial arts film, *The Burning of Red Lotus Temple*, and a new genre was born. The sudden competition forced filmmakers to cut corners; the move imploded on them and the film industry collapsed by the end of the 1920s.

The Kuomintang, which came into power during this era, chose to project modern images of China, and cracked down on martial arts and folktale films. The Lianhua Company, with its slogan of "Revive national cinema," produced films such as *Three Modern Women* (1933) and *New Woman* (1934), highlighting the spirit of social intervention. The left-leaning movement gave birth to films such as *Spring Silkworms* (1933) and *Wild Torrents* (*Kuang Liu*, 1933). This cinema brought the darker, seamier side of society to life and gave expression to the wishes of the people to pursue their dreams as well as to rebel against feudalism and imperialism. China's first horror film, *Singing at Midnight* (1937), also showed a leftist influence. Then World War II broke out and filmmaking went into a chaotic state once more. During this time, patriotic films such as *Mulan Joins the Army* (1939) became very popular.

In the late 1940s, after the war was over, Chinese films and imports from Hollywood such as *Gone with the Wind* competed for viewers' attention. If *Code Name Heaven No. 1*, a spy film, sold 150,000 tickets during its first run in Shanghai, *Gone with the Wind* sold 170,000 during its premiere. For a decade, Hollywood was popular in China. But the Korean War in 1950 put an end to Hollywood's domination. Soviet and Eastern European cinema took its place, and Chinese filmmakers were sent to Moscow to study. By 1952, all private filmmakers were forced to merge under the management of the state.

The new socialist cinema was conceived as an effective propaganda weapon of class struggle, and was devoted to serving the workers, peasants, and soldiers. Filmmakers were motivated to air criticism; many showed their distrust of intellectuals and targeted the party bureaucracy. The confused state of party ideology made some filmmakers choose relatively safer genres such as literary adaptation, opera movies, and war. Notable movies of this period were *The White Haired Girl* (1950), which is considered a classic text of class struggle; *From Victory to Victory* (1952), a war movie that depicted battles between the Kuomintang and the Chinese Communists; and *Liang Shanbo and Zhu Yingtai* (1954), an operatic movie based on the legend of two lovers reunited in death. In the early 1960s, films continued to be made in spite of the restrictions on artistic freedom and strict censorship. Between 1967 and 1969, no films were made. Mao's wife Jiang Qing (ironically, a popular actress during the 1930s) devoted her attention to the staging of the eight model revolutionary plays, and sponsored their filming as a way of displaying them to a larger audience.

During the socialist period, politics reigned supreme over art, and party ideology penetrated everyday life. The planned economy eliminated all market functions. A single state corporation and its provincial branches distributed all films approved by the Film Bureau, theaters showed films as allocated to them, the audience had little effect on production policy, and studios no longer developed distinctive styles or competitive edges. In short, box-office revenues were rarely of concern to artists, cadres, and workers, all of them salaried state employees.[8]

The opening up of China's economy in the 1980s had an immediate impact on the country's film industry, as it did in other fields. Many young directors began making commercial films to entertain audiences. The decade saw three generations of filmmakers in action. The filmmakers of the socialist period—Cheng Yin, Shui Hua, and Cheng Yin—referred to as the "Third Generation," returned to their favorite themes of literary adaptation and revolutionary history. Xie Jin exposed the persecution of the innocent during the Cultural Revolution in *Hibiscus Town* (1986). The Fourth Generation filmmakers studied films but didn't get a chance to direct cinema during the Cultural Revolution. Xie Fei, Huang Jianzhong, and Zheng Dongtian focused on human emotions and took delight in depicting the everyday experiences of ordinary people. They exhibited an eagerness to deal with social issues, and the cinematic landscape was once more infused with artistic inventiveness. Female sexuality became a hot topic, with films such as *A Girl from Hunan* (1986). Women directors such as Zhang Nuanxin and Huang Shuqin explored the theme of female consciousness in *Sacrificed Youth* (1985) and *Woman Demon Human* (1987), respectively. The Fifth Generation filmmakers, whose most notable stars are Zhang Yimou and Chen Kaige, began by challenging the myths of the communist revolution. These filmmakers distinguished themselves by developing a new film language, touching and reinterpreting history from a distance. *One and Eight* (1984) and *Yellow Earth* (1984) blurred the distinction between villains and heroes; at the same time, the spectacular scenery of the Tibetan plateau in *Yellow Earth* helped to convey the depth of cultural tradition.

In 1987, Zhang Yimou made *Red Sorghum* (*Hong Gaoliang*). Based on a novel by Mo Yan, it tells the story of a young woman, played by Gong Li, working at a distillery producing sorghum liquor in a village in Shandong province. With its lush and lusty portrayal of peasant life, the film immediately spearheaded Zhang to the forefront of the Fifth Generation directors. The film picked up the Golden Bear at the Berlin Film Festival in 1988, a critics' award at the Sydney Film Festival, and a Silver Panda at Montreal, and was judged Best Film at the Cuba Film Festival. Suddenly, serving the international market became the Chinese filmmakers' prime obsession. Many young directors adapted their filmmaking to meet the overseas demand for ethnic content, polished narrative, and stylized visuals. Zhang Yimou continued to draw in the crowds and impress the critics with *Raise the Red Lantern* (*Da Hong Denglong Gaogo Gua*), which tells the story of a young woman who becomes one of the concubines of a wealthy man during the warlord era. Chen Kaige shot to fame with *Farewell My Concubine* (*Bawang*

Bie Ji), which depicted the effects of various Chinese political turmoils during the 20th century on a Peking opera troupe. It fetched him a Palme d'Or at Cannes, and the Best Foreign Film award at the Golden Globe Awards in 1993. *Red Firecracker, Green Firecracker* (*Pào Da Shuang Deng*), directed by He Ping, is about a young woman who inherits her father's firecracker factory, falls in love with an itinerant painter even as she is forbidden to marry, and whose life falls into disarray as a result.

The stylized filmmaking of the Fifth Generation found a reaction among the Sixth Generation—a spirited bunch of filmmakers who have chosen an amateur, sometimes documentary style and inspiration in reality, as they attempt to be more truthful to everyday life. Zhang Yuan, Wang Quan'an, Jia Zhangke, and Zhu Wen represent this generation. In the wake of economic reform, the state studios can no longer afford to make experimental films and have switched to commercial genres such as comedy, thrillers, and martial arts. To satisfy their creative urge, the filmmakers of the Sixth Generation have either gone underground or raised money on their own.

Filmmaker Zhang Yuan, with Kate Gong of the Ogilvy Discovery team

Zhang Yuan was born in Nanjing in 1963 and graduated from the Beijing Film Academy in 1989. *Time* magazine named him as one of the world's top 100 leaders in the 21st century. In 1993, he made *Beijing Bastards*, a film without precedent in Chinese cinema. While on the one hand it is a free-form portrait of the rock music generation in the city and their quest for "something to help them live," it is also intertwined with the story of a broken relationship between a young man named Karzi and his pregnant girlfriend. Rock musician Cui Jian plays himself in the film, which veers between fiction and reality. Now with 10 films in the can, Zhang says: "All my films are of completely different styles. Previously, I liked shooting films in a realistic way. *Son and Mama* and *Beijing Bastards*, apart from being feature films, look like documentaries. I've also shot many genuine documentaries, such as *Storms and Stress*. Recently I found a new way to tell a story when I shot the film *Green Tea*. It is a modern love story, and uses the narrative method. The main reason I change my style is because I like to pursue a sense of freshness."

Zhang's filmmaking is always an exercise in inquiry. "I always wonder who we are, where we are from, and where we are going. My friends and I all think of this. Why do we live like this? Why are we the way we are?" It is this spirit of inquiry that allows Zhang to find inspiration in the mundane and the everyday. "Inspiration can come from different directions. Sometimes it can be a piece of news, sometimes something that happens to my friends, or something I find by myself," he says. When asked if he thought foreigners understood what he wanted to express in his movies, he responded: "Foreigners have their own cultural viewpoint in watching movies. But filming language may be the simplest artistic language that lets people from all over the world communicate with each other. Film provides a good opportunity for people to understand each other." His next comment encapsulates the very spirit of creativity in China: "We are in the period of social transformation, so it is the right time for good films to be made in China."

Jia Zhangke attempts to deconstruct his society's dilemmas in a structured way, working in the fashion of a sociologist. In *The*

World (*Shijie*, 2004), he reflects on the problems and challenges of China's transition into the global capitalist market, and shows Chinese society lost in space…If global culture offers a world where everything is connected, accessible, downloadable, and transformable across boundaries, what is the cost of this? Jia's poetic sensibility comes alive in suburban Beijing's 114-acre theme park, *Shijie Gongyuan*, where kitschy replicas of the Eiffel Tower, the Taj Mahal, the Pyramids, and other notable monuments represent a global metropolis. With wit and humor, he explores the environment in which his characters find themselves trapped— by fake architecture, fake costumes (the protagonists are the performers in the theme park's musical spectaculars), and fake emotions. His filmmaking, like that of Zhang Yuan, is innovative. He explains his method thus: "I feel like I learn about the world in small episodes, bits and pieces of life. This is a new narrative method for me to connect everyone together in this film, similar to the way you use a computer—you click here, you click there, each time leading you to another location. This is how the world and its experiences are connected to one another. These small episodes create the big picture, or that's the intention."

Even as his work is austere, there are often musical, indeed theatrical, numbers in his films. They serve a certain purpose, according to Jia: "The musical part of this film, and the theatrical, is a symbol of people escaping from their real lives. Also, a lot of young people in China don't know how to express their emotions, so by creating this artistic–theatrical environment, this mask, they can express themselves more openly. Even though every day they do the same routines at this park, the same dances, it's an escape for them."[9]

My first-ever exposure to Chinese cinema was through Liu Fendou's underground feature *Green Hat* (*Lü Mao Tze*), a euphemistic term, I learned, for a cuckold. A winner of two awards at New York's Tribeca Film Festival, for Best Narrative Feature and Best New Narrative Director, the film is split right down the middle. It is an interwoven comic drama about a heist that goes awry—one of the bank robbers self-destructs upon hearing that his girlfriend has left him—and a domestic drama about the police-man who breaks the heist, his wife, and her lover. "What is love?"

the jilted young man who holds a telephone operator hostage desperately asks the police officer. The question lingers in the middle-aged officer's head as he visits his doctor, who prescribes the popular blue pill to help with his sex life. The middle-aged man takes on layer upon layer of humiliation when he is finally forced to confront his wife's infidelity, his loveless marriage, and the careless swagger of his wife's stud lover. "All along, I thought I was making a romantic film," said Liu Fendou, following a screening of his work. "But the result was far different from my original goal. After my friends watched the movie, they told me they had seen another side of me, which I thought I had forgotten and cured a long time ago. They told me that they could see my pain. I was shocked by their discovery, and yet excited at the same time—they understood me through my movie. The process of making this film was also a process of understanding myself."

While the above directors explore issues and society in contemporary China, the multifaceted Xu Jinglei, introduced at the beginning of this book, chose to step back in time to reverse conventional notions of seduction. Her film *Letter from an Unknown Woman* (2004) is a revisionist version of a Stephan Zweig 1922 novella. Xu paints a picture of an obsessive young girl whose desire for an ever-distant male writer comes to resemble a quest not so much for him to love her, as for him to recognize and acknowledge her existence. The fact that he never does so adds a sense of tragedy, of a wasted *life* rather than a wasted love, which lends the film a melancholy air of loss throughout. By asking the viewer to believe that the young woman could love an openly immoral man who consistently ignores and forgets her, Xu turns the story into an effective character study of a woman struggling to find her own identity. In its stylistic treatment, *Letter* ... has the look of a romantic film, with lush, soft visuals and slow, gliding camerawork, exquisitely observant, indeed celebrating the feminine gaze. It becomes evident that Xu Jinglei injects her own character and gender into the art of filmmaking.

Making the transformation from pop starlet, with a background in commercial TV dramas and cinema such as *Spicy Love Soup* and *Spring Subway*, hasn't been easy for Xu Jinglei. "When I became an actress, people called me a 'flower vase' because they thought of an actress as a hollow, though beautiful, object. At the time, I was very irritated, but now I am happy about it. After all, it means that I am a pretty woman. These days, people call me a 'strong woman.' I don't really see why; I am just pursuing my career independently. So I really don't care about what others say."[10] She explains her many roles—blogger, producer, scriptwriter, actor, singer—as follows: "I have a lot of interests and want to try out everything myself. A director needs to have abundant life experience, otherwise the movie will lack inspiration."

More a one-act play than cinema, Xu Jinglei's third film was released in June 2006. *Dreams May Come* is a conversation between an actress (herself) and a film director, set in one location. One night, while shooting a film, they begin a long conversation, talking about art, values, dreams, and life. They talk and talk, by turns critical, resigned, and confused. Through the two characters' examination of their inner selves, the film represents an outpouring of personal feelings.

In their quest for new themes, and burdened by the need for self-expression, today's filmmakers are turning inward. Contemporary society forms the backdrop for their exploration, but by imbuing their work with a sense of humanity, the filmmakers emphasize the renewal of the Chinese identity—negotiated, evolved, and creative.

As China's entry into the global marketplace accelerated in the 1990s, the country began to gain a modicum of confidence in its potential impact on the cultural landscape. It wasn't enough for brands or products that were made in China to be omnipresent on the shelves of Wal-Mart. The new Chinese ambition was to find a place in Hollywood, in theaters worldwide. It would be a smart way to dispel the notion that the Chinese were skilled at mass production of industrial and consumer goods, but incapable of generating and appreciating creativity.

It took a Taiwanese-born, American-educated man to start that movement. Born in 1954, Ang Lee graduated from the National Taiwan College of Arts in 1975. He moved to the United States to complete a BFA degree in Theater and Theater Direction at the University of Illinois Urbana-Champaign, and a Master's degree in Film Production at New York University. At NYU, he served as assistant director on Spike Lee's student film, *Joe's Bed-Stuy Barbershop: We Cut Heads* (1983). Ten years later, Ang Lee shot to fame with *The Wedding Banquet* (1993), an exploration of cultural and generational conflicts through a homosexual Chinese man who feigns a marriage in order to satisfy the traditional demands of his Taiwanese parents. The film garnered Golden Globe and Oscar nominations, and won a Golden Bear at the Berlin Film Festival. Lee followed this success with *Sense and Sensibility* (1995), his first Hollywood-mainstream movie. It was nominated for Best Feature Film at the Oscars and won Best Adapted Screenplay for the film's screenwriter and lead actress, Emma Thompson. Lee was also voted the year's Best Director by the National Board of Review and the New York Film Critics Circle.

In 2000, Ang Lee came to China and made *Crouching Tiger, Hidden Dragon* (*Wohu Canglong*). The film changed the rules for cinema in China. It launched the blockbuster genre—films that were made at huge expense, and would bring in enormous profits for their producers from both the domestic and international markets, but especially the latter.

The film combined the technical precision of Hollywood with the character pathos of British acting, the noble tradition of a mythical China, and the kinetic grace of Hong Kong's action choreography. Transcending borders, Ang Lee had created a film that was set in China, yet had a universal theme that transcended cultural identity. He had chosen two things that the international audience would find most exotic: a magical representation of imperial China, combined with the Wutan form of martial arts and swordplay.

Crouching Tiger, Hidden Dragon is a timeless story that takes place during the Qing dynasty, when miracles were credible and spirits and gods were present in man's world. It was not unbelievable that zen warriors floated through the air, skimmed the water, and battled in trees and on rooftops. Pain, revenge, and duty are what bind us in this world and are the main plot lines of the film, but in the afterlife love and faith linger on. Plot-wise, *Crouching Tiger, Hidden Dragon* is standard kung fu melodrama: Chow Yun Fat plays Li Mu Bai, a great Wutan warrior. Not only is he burdened with a mission to avenge the death of his Master; he is also bound by honor to deny his love for his best friend, Yu Shu Lien, played by Michelle Yeoh. Mu Bai gives Shu Lien his beloved sword, the Green Destiny, and asks her to deliver it to Sir Te, played by Lung Sihung, a well-respected leader and friend to her father. When Shu Lien visits Sir Te, she meets some of his house-guests, including Jen, played by Zhang Ziyi, the young daughter of a governor who is stuck in a prearranged marriage of which she wants no part. As soon as the sword is placed on display, it is stolen. Everyone assumes this is the doing of Jade Fox, Li Mu Bai's arch-nemesis; but Shu Lien believes Jen is somehow responsible. The story follows Li Mu Bai and Shu Lien's efforts to regain possession of the sword.

Crouching Tiger, Hidden Dragon is visually stunning in more ways than one. It navigates the diverse landscapes of mainland China, from the Gobi Desert to the southern Bamboo Forest to the ancient metropolis of Peking. In addition to the scenery, the strength of the film lies in the human connections. The repressed feelings and emotions of every character in the film put it at the top of Chinese cinema, regardless of the conventional kung fu storyline.

Cinema-goers outside China had never seen anything like it before. *Crouching Tiger, Hidden Dragon* swept the Oscar nominations, eventually winning Best Foreign Language Film, as well as Best Director at the Golden Globes. It became the highest-grossing foreign-language film ever released in the United States.

The international market was suddenly eager. Investors and film directors in China spotted the opportunity. Zhang Yimou, already famous in China, exploded on to the international scene with *Hero* (*Yingxiong*). The film was a lucid and cunning drama: ancient history (third century BC) refracted through a modern skeptic's sensibility. It viewed the birth of a nation through the murky motives of some of the first emperor's potential assassins, who were as duplicitous in their emotional lives as in their fatal politics. The plot is a series of tales told by the warrior Nameless, played by Jet Li, to the Qin king (Chen Daoming). Nameless has three main adversaries: Sky (Donnie Yen), a master martial artist whom he defeats in the film's first, superb battle scene; Broken Sword (Tony Leung Chiu-wai), a calligrapher who is as adroit with a brush as with a saber; and Flying Snow (Maggie Cheung), Broken Sword's soul mate. Flying Snow has a side skirmish of her own with Moon, played by Zhang Ziyi, who is Broken Sword's smitten apprentice. Loyalties are tested, alliances made and sundered. Death is the price the warrior has to pay for betrayal of the king or the heart.

Released in October 2002, *Hero* quickly became the highest-grossing film in the history of Chinese cinema. Zhang Yimou recalled his inspiration and his early attempts to make Wuxia (martial arts literature) films. "I always enjoyed Wuxia...I read my first Wuxia novel in the 1960's. It was called *Hawk Claw King*. I always wanted to make a Wuxia movie. Several years ago, I started to work on the script of *Hero*. At that time, I wanted to adopt one of Louis Cha's or Gu Long's stories. I hoped that someone would make the film once the script was done, but I failed. Then Ang Lee's *Crouching Tiger, Hidden Dragon* became a hit. We started ahead, and now they say we try to imitate Ang Lee." Zhang Yimou acknowledges the impact of *Crouching Tiger, Hidden Dragon*: "*Crouching Tiger, Hidden Dragon* has positively influenced the market. It created a very big market. The west is very interested in this subject and we can have plenty of room to stretch." He articulates the need for the worldwide market: "We need the international market. The budget is high. To make sure the boss (investor) makes money, only focusing on the domestic market is not enough."[11]

In 2005, Chen Kaige took up the gauntlet with *The Promise*. In the film, he combined the artistic vision of Tim Yip, who won an Oscar for art direction for his work on *Crouching Tiger, Hidden Dragon*, and the special effects wizardry of Centro Digital Pictures, whose credits include Quentin Tarantino's *Kill Bill* films, to create breathtaking visuals that completely overshadowed a long-winded plot. By the time Zhang Yimou came up with his Tang dynasty-inspired *Curse of the Golden Flower* in early 2007, the cinema audiences in both China and the West were beginning to tire. The excessive attention to costume drama—for *Curse*...3,000 handmade costumes were tailored by 40 Chinese seamstresses and embroiderers at a cost of US$1.3 million—and special effects-enabled martial arts had cinema–goers clamoring for new fare. The talking point of *Curse...* was no longer its lavish cinematography or Liu Ye's acting, but the voluptuous, bosom-revealing style of the gowns and the golden phoenix headdress worn by Gong Li.

The excesses of the imperial costume dramas and martial arts spectaculars created a void in the market. Ning Hao stepped right into it with his low-budget, action-packed fare. With *Crazy Stone*, the 30-year-old director, whose two previous works—*Incense* and *Mongolian Pingpong*—had both played at several international film festivals, with the former winning the Grand Prize at Tokyo Filmex in 2003, turned his hand to criminal farce to great effect, weaving a tangled web of blundering theft and misunderstandings. *Crazy Stone* begins with the discovery of a priceless jade stone at a dilapidated factory that is on the verge of being demolished by a greedy property developer. Seeing the stone as a means of making money, the factory owner decides to put it on show in a rundown temple while he tries to find a buyer, appointing factory worker and ex-detective Bao, played by Guo Tao, as chief of security. The poor man, already suffering from prostrate troubles, soon has his hands full as an incompetent trio of thieves, a professional burglar hired by the unscrupulous developer, and the factory owner's slimy son try all kinds of tricky schemes to get their hands on the stone.

The film is very funny, both in terms of clever dialogue and situations, as well as in its use of broad physical humor. However, Ning never lets things go over-the-top; although there is plenty of slapstick, the film never strays from its believable and engaging scenario. There are a great many laugh-out-loud moments, especially toward the end as the characters very slowly come to see the bigger picture, leading to some amusing resolutions. Ning Hao's superb direction employs a variety of technical tricks, including split screen work and some inventive editing, all of which complement the narrative rather than simply being included for the sake of it. He keeps things moving at a frenzied pace, with plenty of action and fiendishly designed set pieces to raise the viewer's pulse. Although there are a few brief bursts of violence, the tone is generally kept playful, allowing Ning to give the film its own identity, as opposed to simply going down the usual gritty, hardboiled robbery-gone-wrong route.

For a low-budget production, the film created a genuine sensation at the Chinese box office, raking in more than RMB17 million (over US$2 million). Unlike some of his predecessors, Ning Hao has enjoyed the advantage of being exposed to Western cinema, even as he remained within China. "I have to admit that both Quentin Tarantino and Guy Ritchie are my filmmaking teachers. *Crazy Stone* belongs to the same category as their films," he says. The Shaanxi province native finds his plots in everyday life. "I always think that in China, more imaginative things usually happen in a mid-sized city."[12]

Beijing-based producer Lola is also returning to explore her roots in Yunnan province. The Yunnan Film Project, which she launched, is a series of 10 independent low-budget films, all directed by women directors. Not everyone among them was a filmmaker—there is an installation artist, a poet, a musician, and an experimental stage actress. Between them, they are producing dark comedy, psychological thrillers, and historical dramas. Lola handpicked the directors on the basis of their previous work; Zhang Cheng, for example, co-wrote *Crazy Stone*; while Wang Fen directed *The Case*, a surreal tale about a man who finds a suitcase with the body parts of a woman frozen into ice blocks. The film is already impressing critics, picking up awards at the Shanghai International Film Festival in 2007. Wang Fen says, "I was...struck by the intrinsic danger of this seemingly peaceful place—so much of what was beautiful was also dangerous, like avalanches and river rapids. Very quickly, a new story grew out of these impressions."[13]

Ang Lee has continued to make waves, both with his filmmaking and accolades. In 2007, he served up *Lust, Caution* (*Se Jie*), which challenged the limits of Chinese cinema once again. The sexually charged spy thriller is based on a short story by the writer Eileen Chang, and is set in the early 1940s during the Sino-Japanese war, mostly in Japanese-occupied Shanghai. Eileen Chang had a foot in two worlds. Her celebrated early stories and novellas, written in the 1940s, evoked the heady, glamorous fusion of East and West, old and new, which characterized Shanghai before the communist takeover. *Lust, Caution* was inspired by an actual assassination plot in the 1930s, incorporated elements of Chang's own life: a university education in Hong Kong interrupted by war, and a doomed romance with an older man publicly known as a traitor. Chang's first husband, the writer Hu Lancheng, briefly served in the puppet government and was an inveterate philanderer. In the film, the heroine, Chia Chi (played by Tang Wei), belongs to a university drama troupe plotting to assassinate a collaborator named Yee (played by Tony Leung). Assigned to seduce the target, an official in the puppet government, she falls into a desperately physical affair, driven by both passion and suspicion. To expand Chang's slender story to a feature-length script, Lee worked with Wang Huiling, his co-writer on *Crouching Tiger, Hidden Dragon*.

Even as *Lust, Caution* was a brilliant film, scooping up the Golden Globe at the Venice Film Festival exactly two years after Lee's win for *Brokeback Mountain*, and sweeping the Golden Horse Awards in Taiwan, winning seven—including Best Film and Best Director, the brouhaha and interest around this film remained centered on its explicit sex scenes. According to Ang Lee, the scenes were an essential part of the film, not a device to attract viewers or undue attention. "They're like the fight sequences in '*Crouching Tiger*,'" he said. "It's life and death. It's where they really show their character." He added, "And it's part of the plot, since it's all about acting, levels of acting. You're performing when you have sex."[14]

When the film was released in mainland China, these scenes were deleted to conform with the censorship regulations. However, it very soon became evident that the Chinese cinemagoer had matured and was willing to challenge those regulations. Dong Yanbin, a PhD student at the China University of Political Science and Law in Beijing, filed a suit against the nation's film censor, the State Administration of Radio, Film and Television (SARFT), for infringing upon his "consumer rights," reported the *Beijing Times*. "I felt greatly disappointed after seeing the movie," the paper quoted Dong as saying. "Compared to Eileen Chang's original, the incomplete structure of *Lust, Caution* and fragmented portrayal of the female lead's psyche make it hard for the audience to appreciate the movie's art."

If, on the one hand, Ang Lee has been able to make the world sit up and take notice of Chinese cinema and stories, on the other hand he has compelled the audience and the regulators to re-evaluate the norms and boundaries of creativity within China.

It is evident from the multiplicity of themes, styles, and sources of inspiration in the last decade that Chinese cinema has attained a level of creative maturity and craft that is comparable to anywhere in the worldwide market. The relatively lower level of recognition at the Oscars is more the result of the awards being "all American games, established by Americans to critique American productions …they only have one category for all of international cinema," said Zhang Yimou. "I would be rather thrilled if one day a Chinese cinema award can amass so much power and influence."[15]

With the explosion of digital video (DV) technology since around 2002, many young film enthusiasts are now able to realize their dreams of expressing their individual creativity in China. The New Documentary Movement (*Xin Jilu Yundong*) in China is the combined result of a number of factors: a general mixed sense of hope and loss in an era of dramatic change; greater freedom in the economic sector, combined with some freedom of expression; and the free availability of technology to shoot and air the films. In 2006, Hu Ge shot a hilarious spoof of Chinese director Chen Kaige's *The Promise*. Hu turned it into a 20-minute TV crime drama titled *A Murder Sparked by a Chinese Bun* and posted it online. It was the talk of the Internet for weeks, but it also outraged the director, who threatened to sue Hu.

The DV filmmakers explore themes and look for drama in everyday life. Twenty-two-year-old Huang Kai studied film art at Shanghai University and now works as an editor with Shanghai TV. His eerie 15-minute film *And I Knew* explores homosexuality and includes a bittersweet love triangle; while *East-South-West-North* depicts a delicate and complicated sexual relationship on the university campus. Both films have picked up awards in China. Huang's classmates worked with him as producers, cameramen, makeup artists, and art directors. But it isn't sexuality alone that interests Huang. In *Doctor City*, he tells the story of Wang Beibei, a white-collar worker who lives a busy but monotonous, lonely life. Huang explained, "The story deals with aphasia, a psychological disorder common in urban life. The sufferers have decent jobs, but are overwhelmed by the nameless feeling of loneliness. Their ability to communicate with others is weakened by living in a bustling metropolis."

Yang Jian, another postgraduate student, directed a 19-minute horror film, *W.C.* He was inspired by his own experience as a child. "The toilet of my home was dark and shabby, and it was easy to imagine things. I often thought there was a ghost behind me," he said with a chuckle. *DV China* (2002), a film by Zheng Dasheng, goes upcountry to come up with a remarkable story. Since the early 1990s, the villagers in Jindezheng, led by Zhou Yuanqiang, creative director of the local cultural center, have learned all the techniques of film production: scriptwriting, casting, shooting, montage, and even special effects. With great enthusiasm they produced 18 serials, although they lacked equipment and were short on budget. The energetic director then initiated a new challenge for his enthusiastic and amateur actors: their first kung fu serial. The documentary followed the production of this new serial and their difficulties with fund-raising, resolving technical problems, and interpersonal relations among themselves.

Guangzhou-based Huang Weikai's first film, *Floating* (2005), is a slice-of-life documentary about a young guitarist named Yang Jiwei who plies his trade in the pedestrian underpasses of Guangzhou's central business district. The camera traces Yang as he drifts through two years of his life. It deals unflinchingly with sex, survival, suicide, social discrimination, abortion, and police detention. After graduating from art school in 1995, Huang tried to get as close as possible to film. This wasn't easy in China in the days before things went digital. First, he offered his services free to Guangzhou's only production studio. When that plan failed, he called every cinema in the local Yellow Pages. "I decided a movie theater was the next best thing. That way I could at least watch movies every day," he says. In 1997, Huang found a job as a graphic designer and devoted his spare time to writing screenplays. The only problem was that no one would read them. Just as he was making a last-ditch effort by applying to film schools, digital video hit China and changed all the equations. "The more I learned about DV, the more film school seemed unnecessary. You spend a lot of time with subjects that are of no use to a filmmaker, like politics and English. I thought that was a huge waste of time. It was better just to buy a DV and do it myself."

The shift to DV and the growing richness of independent films in China has prompted comparisons with the French New Wave of the 1960s, when the advent of lightweight cameras and faster film stock brought a new generation of filmmakers out of the studio and into the world. "There is a new kind of freedom emerging for Chinese filmmakers. They don't trust institutions. They occupy a new space of creativity," says Barbara Keifenheim, a filmmaker and anthropologist who served as a judge at the 2007 Yunnan Multi-Cultural Visual Forum, or YunFest, where Huang's *Floating* made its first appearance among scores of other DV films. "It's a bit reminiscent of the 1960s in Western countries," she says. Young filmmakers have found this new creative space outside the confines of China's mainstream media and its apparatus of state control, says Lu Xinyu, a professor of journalism at Shanghai's Fudan University and author of *Documenting China: The Contemporary Documentary Movement in China*. "They don't go through any of the official production channels recognized by the state. In this way they escape scrutiny." Many of these films are strikingly candid in their depiction of Chinese society. Their motivation for truth-seeking, says Lu, is at least in part a reaction against the false images and idealized views projected by the media and mainstream cinema.[16]

These films are also a reaction against the state-approved documentaries of the 1980s and 1990s, which took a top-down perspective on Chinese life. Young filmmakers today are far more interested in letting their subjects speak for themselves. "The difference between filmmakers today and those in the past is that they want to enter into and examine the lowest levels of Chinese society," says Lu Cheng Long, a 23-year-old engineering student in the northern Chinese city of Harbin and director of *The Ice Men*, agreeing that there has been a dramatic shift in perspective. "Before, directors would make grand films or documentaries about eminent scientists or other model characters. Now we care much more about the lives of ordinary people." Cheng's own first film, which takes a behind-the-scenes look at the famous ice carvers who work their magic each year at Harbin's grand Ice Festival, is a good case in point. On the other hand, there are some who are simply having fun with film. Nie Sulin, an 18-year-old international trade major at the Sichuan Business Vocational College, became a celebrity on the Web when he uploaded his amusing adaptation of animal dances as an entry to the 7-Up 'I Lemon You' Music Video contest. The mashup trailer remixed the funny postures of animals such as a cat, bear, parrot, and mouse, taken from animal documentaries, and set it to music. Nie Sulin now plans to make an original short Web film.

I believe that the DV movement in China will throw up an incredible variety five years from now. Filmmakers working in this medium will touch on important social topics not addressed by the mainstream media. There will also be lots of very personal films, with young directors exploring their own lives. They will be, indeed, the new progenitors of creativity in China.

1   Benjamin Joffe-Walt, "Mad About the Girl—A Pop Idol in China," *The Guardian*, October 7, 2005.

2   Xu Wei, "Win!Win!Win! We Have Three Heroes!" *Shanghai Daily*, July 23, 2007.

3   Wang Yong, "At Last a Manly Man Who Can Sing Trumps Girly Boys," *Shanghai Daily*, July 17, 2007.

4   Yin Hong, "Meaning, Production, Consumption: The History and Reality of Television Drama in China," in S.H. Donald, M. Keane, and Yin Hong (eds), *Media in China: Consumption, Content and Crisis* (London: Routledge Curzon, 2002).

5   Michael A. Keane, "Television Drama in China: Remaking the Market," *Culture and Policy*, 115, 2005.

6   Sheldon H. Lu, "Soap Opera in China—The Transnational Politics of Visuality, Sexuality and Masculinity," *Cinema Journal*, 40(1), Fall 2000.

7   Zhu Ying, "Chinese TV Dramas—Will Confucius Save the Day?" *Asia Media*, February 7, 2006.

8   Yingjin Zhang, "A Centennial Review of Chinese Cinema, 2003," http://chinesecinema.ucsd.edu/essay_ccwlc.html.

9   Jia Zhangke was interviewed by David Walsh on September 29, 2004, at the Toronto Film Festival. www.wsws.org/articles/2004/sep2004/int-s29.shtml.

10 Thomas Podvin, "Declaration of Independence," *That's Shanghai*, August 2006.

11 www.monkeypeaches.com/hero/interview01.html.

12 Yu Senlu, "Snatching the Stone," *City Weekend*, July 20–August 2, 2006, Shanghai.

13 From an interview with Carl Thelin, "Strength in Numbers," *That's Shanghai*, October 2007.

14 Dennis Lim, "In Ang Lee's *Lust, Caution*, Love is Beautiful to See, Impossible to Hold," *International Herald Tribune*, August 27, 2007.

15 "The Bombastic and the Beautiful: An Interview with Director Zhang Yimou, by Artemisia Ng," *Asia-Pacific Arts Magazine*, December 21, 2006.

16 www.supernaut.info/2005/08/crazy_for_digital.html.

Designed for Success
Products and fashion embrace creativity and set cash registers ringing

"Design is the way companies improve their competitiveness."

Yu Zida, Vice President, Haier Group

Yali Ling's elaborate costumes

In May 2000, *BusinessWeek* carried an article headlined, "A Legend for How Long?" The magazine's correspondent wrote about the success of computer manufacturer Legend Corporation, but questioned how long the company would be able to sustain its leadership, especially after China's accession to the World Trade Organization. The article concluded, "[If] Legend's young managers don't get the mix right, customer Qi's next PC may well be—gulp—a Dell."[1]

Five years later, the same publication announced the arrival of China on the world's product design scene with a cover: "China Design." Legend, renamed Lenovo in 2003, was hailed as a company where a renaissance had taken place. How the opinion had changed!

The turnaround year was 1998, driven by the company's ambition to become a global player. Design would play a central role in the company's ability to compete and stay ahead of the game. After two years of intensive R&D, during which the company embarked on an exercise to understand better the needs of the Chinese consumer, and collaborated with world leaders in design, such as Palo Alto, California-based IDEO and Portland, Oregon-based Ziba, and in materials, such as Nike and GE Plastics, Legend launched the Tianxi laptop. The pastel-colored, shell-shaped, Internet-ready computer was an instant hit. The business model of melding the consumer appetite for design, supporting the design with innovative technology, and rounding off the package with smart marketing—such as a year's free Internet access provided by China Mobile—made the company the undisputed leader in China's personal computer market.

I met Yao Yingjia, the executive director of Lenovo's Innovation Design Center, at his office in Beijing's Silicon Valley, Haidian District. Since 2002, Yao and his team—which has grown to 80 designers—have been churning out new, sometimes revolutionary technology designs with great commercial success and design-world acclaim. "Creativity and design are really important for Lenovo," he began. "But I believe that design is not only for the product. You may design for the product, but you also design for the people who would use it, for the organization, and for the industry. Our chairman, Li Yuanqing, is also a designer, but he focuses on organization design. That is a key step that gives rise to a culture of creativity within Lenovo." One of Yao's key tasks, when he took over, was to break down the rigid Confucian hierarchy that inhibits innovation in many Chinese companies. In the design center's "war room" and out in people's homes, marketplaces, and villages, his team soaks in the culture of technology use. They travel to museums to understand what is blooming in the art market. "I don't believe in giving my team too much direction. If you give your team direction, you won't be surprised. As a manager, I like surprises," he said, his views sounding almost antithetical to established norms of management.

Many of Lenovo's new designs are the result of combining today's cutting-edge technology with elements from China's traditional culture. For instance, a Lenovo speakerphone was inspired by the traditional Chinese hotpot meal—where families place the bubbling pot in the center of the dining table and share the meal. The red-and-black phone, which resembles a dish, comes with a remote control balanced in the center.

"Culture gives us those flashes of inspiration," said Yao. But in order to be a global player, the inspiration need not always be Chinese. "We have this designer from New Zealand who does a lot of running, goes to the gym regularly, and is also into yoga. We were brainstorming about a new laptop and she came up with this idea about a really flexible and beautifully poised laptop," Yao said. The concept for the Yoga laptop is hinged on the bending of the mind. The design harmonized the personality of the user with the object of use. The design of this multifunctional laptop was realized through the inclusion of an innovative soft hinge technology support that allowed for three modes of self-locking position: as a general laptop, tilted at a 300-degree angle; as a tablet display screen; and bent over at a 360-degree angle as a drawing pad. In keeping with the flexibility of use and transport, the Yoga laptop was designed with a detachable keyboard and wireless mouse. Finished in tactile leather material, it had an inherent built-in visual identity technology programmed to automatically identify its owner, making it personal and secure. No small wonder that the Yoga laptop picked up the Red Dot design award from the German design institute Design Zentrum Nordrhein Westfalen for Best of the Best for Highest Design Quality.

For Lenovo, the design awards have been as frequent as the rises in its bottom line. In 2003, Lenovo won four influential design awards, including the Japan G-Mark International Design Award, the German IF International Design Award, *CHIPS* magazine's Annual Product Award at CEBIT, as well as the Hong Kong Design Centre's Best China Design Award. The Industrial Designers Society of America (IDSA), which recognizes the "best of the best from the U.S., Asia, and Europe," awarded the ET960 smart phone for its design. But Lenovo didn't stop at innovating with its product alone. The Institute of Packaging Professionals in the United States recognized Lenovo with the 2006 AmeriStar Award in the electronics packaging category for the Lenovo Desktop PC Reflex thermoformed cushion design. The Lenovo Desktop PC pack eliminated the use of traditional PC foam packaging and decreased by 25% per PC the amount of materials required to effectively ship Lenovo desktop PCs. The new, completely recycled, and recyclable Desktop PC pack is helping to significantly reduce the use of virgin plastic required in the production of traditional foam packaging.

Yao's confidence in his team's design abilities prompted him to enter the competition to design the 2008 Olympic Torch. Why remain confined to technology products, he thought? Lenovo's design was chosen from over 300 entries from all over the world. It was a historic moment for the company.

"The torch design took ten months and was the product of more than 30 engineers and design specialists," Yao explained in his blog. "In the design of the 2008 Olympic torch, cultural elements play a very important role in this innovative project. Like any other project, we started with a brain-storming discussion. Designers were very active and proposed many good suggestions, including lots of Chinese cultural elements—among those dragon, lantern and cloud pattern were the most representative ones. But, which one could perfectly embody the Chinese culture, Olympics spirit and the hopes and dreams of the people? In Chinese history the dragon is the symbol of imperial authority, while the cloud is the symbol for the public will, symbolizing the spirit of sharing and equality. Unconsciously, the cloud pattern has deeply penetrated into every corner of our life; it exists everywhere and so ubiquitously that we are sometimes insensitive to its omnipresence. There are also a lot of cloud patterns in traditional Chinese architectures, sculptures, vessels and paintings. We all finally agreed to choose the cloud pattern.

The Olympic Torch, designed by Lenovo

In traditional Chinese culture, the image of Dragon and Phoenix indicates auspicious things and fine blessings. A necessary element in depicting their images is the cloud, which harmonies and enhances the atmosphere through which they fly. Clouds were created among the earth and heaven. In Chinese aesthetics, cloud reflects nature and the human spirit. Cloud is also the most important element in Chinese traditional paintings. Cloud can merge, scatter, generate or disappear, always in endless cycles and constantly changing form. In Chinese culture, cloud is really quite magical. It generates a new creature by merging together. In the Olympics, with people coming from different nationalities and races to meet together, to share together and create a new future together, we felt cloud is the very element which conforms perfectly to the Olympic spirit."[2]

The "cloud of promise" design was far more culture-oriented than most other Lenovo designs. Yao hopes this cloud design will integrate Chinese culture, the Olympic spirit, and the future hopes and dreams of people around the world, dreams that are embodied by the Olympic Games and their celebration of excellence and achievement.

It was evident that Lenovo's global ambitions were being realized, and not just through actions such as taking over IBM's PC business in 2005. By May 2007, the company's net profit had rocketed, the first sign that the company had begun to turn round the former IBM PC unit. Full-year profit increased 625% to US$161 million, compared with US$22 million the previous year. "China throughout the year was just stunning," said William Amelio, Lenovo's chief executive. "But the big turnaround was the Americas."

Consumer electronics giant Haier recognizes the importance of design as it pursues an aggressive worldwide expansion plan. Haier exports to 160 countries. Some 120 industrial designers and 25 consumer researchers study the unique needs of consumers in different markets. The company spends 6% of its sales income on R&D. In Saudi Arabia, Haier discovered that people needed extra-large washing machines to wash their bulky robes. They began selling a machine with a six-kilogram wash tub, but it didn't do very well; so they increased the size to nine kilograms. The product still languished in the stores. It was only when they launched a mammoth 12-kilogram machine, that the product became a hit—10,000 units flew out of stores every month. In India, washing machines were tailor-made to handle the voltage fluctuations and power outages that characterize many towns; the machine takes off from where it left when the power goes off. The company realized that U.S. college students who live in small spaces try to optimize every bit of their available space. They introduced a small refrigerator that doubled as a tabletop that students could use to eat at or write on. Haier's strength in innovation is evidenced by the 7,000-plus patents its design and R&D teams have won.

It seems clear that the world is gearing up for a well-designed, innovative brand from China. For many, the rise of China as a creative power is surprising, partly because it seems to rob many economies of their sole, surviving competitive advantage. This rise, however, is by no means accidental. It is the imperative that many companies have come to embrace, with no small impetus from the central government.

Hu Shuhua, head of the product innovation management center at the Wuhan Institute of Technology, says: "Innovation is an overall strategy for maintaining China's economic security. Now is the time for us to innovate … we have the economic and technical base to do it." Moses Cheng, senior partner at the Hong Kong-based solicitors P.C. Woo, adds: "Design is a necessity, rather than a luxury, in the foreseeable future. I would say that design is a requirement for survival, rather than the traditional belief that it only adds value to whatever you are doing right now."

The push for Chinese companies to become more creative comes as much from the consumption landscape as from above. The government has set up the Creative China Industrial Alliance, under the Ministry of Information Industry, with the explicit mandate to push the slogan "Created in China." Su Tong is its founding executive director. Sounding apologetic about the mistakes of the past, especially the focus on mass production, he says: "For a long time, we liked to use the term 'material productivity.' An example of such an attitude is the slogan 'The crop from the field is as great as the effort can yield.' This focus on production and performance indicators in China impacted negatively on creativity. Also, the period of feudal despotism that prevailed for so long allowed the ruling class to suppress grassroots creativity. This introduced another gene: one that emphasized rigidity, autocracy, the suppression of individuality, and the discounting of initiative. But now, more and more people who are working in education and the government have come to a common understanding of creativity. Expressions such as 'respect the original creativity of the ordinary people' have surfaced in high-level communication." In China, once there is a political will, things happen.

Even as the leaders acknowledge that the development of creative industries is an international activity and that China is eager to learn from other nations, implicit in their efforts is an exploration into and preservation of China's own cultural heritage and, in the words of Su Tong, "liberating the creative gene of Chinese culture." In its June 4, 2007, cover story, *Fortune* magazine had as its headline: "China's New Cultural Revolution: How after years of embracing all things Western, Chinese consumers are turning...more Chinese." While driving Starbucks out of the Forbidden City is just one manifestation of this newfound cultural pride, it is accompanied by the rising popularity of outlets such as the Sichuan-themed South Beauty chain of restaurants, dishes from which have featured on the pages of *Vogue* magazine.

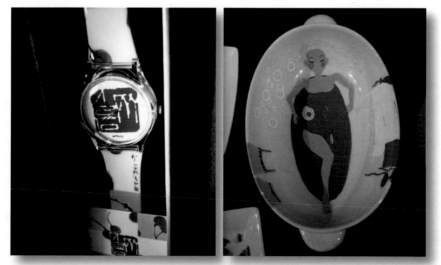

Everyday objects imbued with design: a watch by ArtKey, and a soap dish by students of Shanghai Normal University

The seeds of this transformation are indeed being sown at the grassroots level, and by addressing a basic issue—the shortage of talent. China's first design school opened at Hunan University in Changsha province in 1982. Today, there are 450 design schools. They are "popping up like bamboo shoots," in the words of Yan Yang, the dean of the Industrial Design Center at Beijing's Tsinghua University. Collectively, these schools graduate about 10,000 students a year. Supremely confident students from the Art and Design Academy at Zhejiang Sci-tech University participate in design shows such as the Shanghai International Creative Industry Week, rubbing shoulders with top designers from Europe. One of the designs that they have showcased is the Ding microwave oven. Designed by Weike Zhu, not only does it revolutionize the box-shaped design of microwave ovens that currently dominates the market, but it also evokes childhood memories of constructing an oven during a picnic. (The traditional clay oven was cylindrical in shape.)

"We hope that our students can influence the economy and culture of China," Yang told us. He is a strong advocate of the belief that design should be for everyone; that it should benefit the common people—something that many designers haven't been doing. He illustrated his belief as follows:

"Bentley and Porsche are such well-designed cars. But no matter how well you design them, the number of people benefiting from their design couldn't possibly be more than half a million around the world. On the other hand, if you put some time, money, and thought into designing a better farm truck, half a *billion* people would benefit from it. You would make less money per truck, but just imagine the total economic and social value!"

A microwave oven in the shape of a traditional Chinese cooker, designed by students of Zhejiang University

Yang spoke of the challenges facing design education, and of the evolution of the industry to date:

"Our seniors all studied abroad and brought the most advanced design ideas from Germany, Japan, and other countries. We viewed the design situation in China from their perspective, and it all seemed so backward 30, 40 years ago. The distance between the level of design in foreign countries and in China was so large that we felt we couldn't bridge it. Then, in the 1980s, the leaders in design education began to spend time propagating the very idea of design. But no one in business, the government, or society understood them. From 1998, things changed. Big companies like Haier, Lenovo, TCL, Konka, Hisense, and Huawei changed overnight. As the demand for their products built, they learned that design was essential to their business and began employing both domestic and foreign designers."

Until the late 1990s, the role of the designer as a problem-solver in the entire development process, and as a conceptual resource, was underestimated. "Twenty years ago, the designer in China was called an art designer, whose job was to decorate the product and make models after the engineer had finished 95% of the product. It was a pure business purpose—intended to satisfy the need of the consumer, who was beginning to want new and beautiful products. What we've been able to introduce into design education is an understanding of the situation in which the product will be used and the feeling that people have when they are using it, and thereby make the case for the designer to get involved more deeply, much earlier," Yang explained.

s.point design is one company which insists on the designer's deep involvement. "The design team is a part of a larger whole, often a connection between the various departments. To succeed, designers need to understand the company's goals and strategies. The designer's activities revolve around the business strategies of the company," explains Zhou Yi, who founded the company in 1997. We met him at s.point's office in a red industrial building in the northwest of Shanghai's city center; on another occasion, I met his German vice president, Tim Richter, for an engaging conversation, especially about why he chose to come to China to work in design, rather than go to the United States. Richter was quite candid: China was a clean palette to work with. On three floors, in an inspiring and bright space covering more than 750 square meters, including room for design, research, and engineering teams, a model-making workshop, color and materials lab, a product showroom, and generous areas for meetings and brainstorming sessions, a multicultural team of 40 designers cranks out prototypes for a range of multinational and Chinese companies. This mix of designers representing different cultures and disciplines helps determine the needs of both local and international markets. Zhou Yi's assertion is confident: "We are not a Chinese design company. We are a design company that is based in China." And one reason that s.point is flourishing is because some companies feel the need to locate their design and innovation centers close to their factories. "In order to survive, a company must be highly responsive to market changes, and designers must be able to make fast and accurate decisions. To remain competitive with the fast pace of technological changes and improvements, a design should be continually updated, even if it is successful in the market," says the company's publication, *Designing Tomorrow*, which sets out its philosophy and practice. "Mobile phone companies churn out forty new models a year, and manufacture a heck of a lot of their phones in China. The revolutionary new models like the Moto Razr come once every couple of years. The rest is merely tinkering with the design. It is much faster and, of course, cheaper to do that incremental innovation here." s.point counts Motorola and Panasonic among its clients. "To be number one here, you have to do international design jobs," Zhou Yi stresses.

Tim Richter (extreme left), of s.point design, walks visitors around his office

Zhou Yi and his team are acutely aware of the role of design in furthering business goals. s.point believes in "honest design," which is the truthful reflection of a brand and aims to convey the brand's values to its customers, not to mislead through extravagant, useless styling. Honest design, they say, should not only be for products but should permeate into everyday lives to be fully appreciated. "An important evaluation of design is its cost-effectiveness. Achieving cost-effectiveness is a team effort that can be a guiding goal throughout the entire design process. Having a good design strategy laid out for a company does save a lot of money."[3]

s.point's flexible PC

One of s.point's truly innovative designs was the Dragonfly water dispensing system. Hyflux is a world leader in water treatment, having undertaken large-scale industrial and urban projects in Singapore, China, and the Middle East. The company is founded on the realization that our key source of life, water, is exposed to innumerable dangers and that impurities in our resources need to be removed to create cleaner, healthier, and better-tasting drinking water. The Dragonfly water generator does something quite extraordinary: it draws water from the atmosphere, using a membrane filtration technology, completely eliminating the need for refilling. s.point's engineers and designers flung aside traditional conventions about water dispensers and refigured the internal components to better address water generation, filtration, and heat dissipation. The Dragonfly's materials were unlike most dispensers in the market; the specially processed translucent polypropylene and stainless steel conveyed the product's simple function and innovative technology. The design language used showcased the high technology and conveyed Hyflux's superior brand image as a water-conscious company, not merely as a manufacturer of water dispensers.

s.point's work for Intel Corporation was based on the belief that people are not affected by innovations in technology that occur in the research laboratory; they are affected only when the technology is realized in a form that is useful and when the context of use is taken into account. The children's PC developed by s.point aimed to educate as well as entertain, in addition to providing a new way of interfacing with new technology. The design research team observed children using computers in order to understand their habits and unfulfilled usage requirements. They studied where they used computers, their ability to operate them, their frequency and time of usage, the functions most often used, and other behaviors, such as eating in front of the computer. It was observed that parents regarded the computer as an investment for the child's education; at the same time, they were worried about the content that the child might access over the Internet. The children's PC was designed to meet the different user modes—reading, writing, and interactivity: placed on a spherical base, and using a bearing structure, the screen could be rotated into different positions and angles. A "Rug" accessory allowed children to draw, doodle, and write, as ultrasonic technology collected the data in real time. A physical lock allowed parents to control children's access to the computer. The children's PC, which went to market quite successfully, illustrates the role that design can play between technology and the end-user.

Like s.point, mooma design agency is driven by an "unnatural obsession with understanding people, brands and technology."[4] The firm believes in combining scientific precision with aesthetics. Thirty designers with experience spanning medical instruments, home appliances, and furniture design, and educated in the best design schools in China and overseas, imbue mooma with a creative energy that is manifest in every project or assignment. Ding Hua, head of industrial design, studied at Tsinghua University; Hou Zhengguang and Luigi Laurenzi, an Italian by birth, were classmates in the United Kingdom. "Furniture design is a fresh, young area in China," says Hou. "In this starting phase, we need some foreigners —their industry is quite mature and they know all the processes. It's quicker this way; you can figure it out yourself, but that's not necessary." Hou is evidently in a hurry to make a mark. mooma recognizes the need to differentiate its products, touting the philosophy "Get a mice into Mickey Mouse," or attracting attention through emphasizing differentiation. "Winning attention is winning profits," Hou explains.

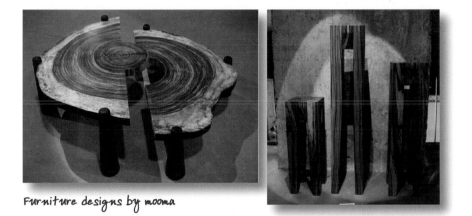

Furniture designs by mooma

Some of that attention is gained through the management of details. "Detail means everything to us. It infiltrates every design element, form, color, material, and so on," says Hou. A baby scale designed by mooma reflects every aspect of a child's behavior and preferences—the form itself is childlike, the colors are bright and enticing. A product's compatibility with the culture often determines its final design. The Bamboo series of lighting is an example. "People in China are familiar with bamboo, which is very Oriental and light. But we didn't want to make it like folk craft. We combined it with metal to give it a very contemporary feel." Other lamps are inspired by birdcages. A traditional foot massage basin has been redesigned and reinterpreted in a modern context, even as a bigger curve in its design creates a more enjoyable user experience. This cultural immersion allows mooma to conjure up new products, and to cater to previously unexpressed needs. As people are becoming more concerned with hygiene and food quality, the firm created a vegetable washing machine that effectively eliminates dirt and pesticide residue from the vegetables, as well as a disinfectant cabinet, for its client Yinghua Hygiene Products.

Other product designs are based on usage environments. The Huihan Technologies Wi-Fi "Liftless" phone solves the problem of picking up the phone while driving. A radar gun developed for Xian Biken Technology is designed like a large-bore shotgun, forbidding in its looks, but nicely balanced so that a police officer who wields it for any length of time doesn't end up with aching hands. International clients such as Otis Elevator Company work with mooma to understand the specific contexts of use of its products in China, and remodel them accordingly. First impressions matter, and as the elevator is a key element in creating a first impression in commercial buildings, must, mooma believes, be designed well.

Both s.point design and mooma design have realized the importance of creativity in furthering their business objectives, but this realization is built on the growing demand for better-designed products in China and elsewhere. Such consumer demand has spurred the business of art licensing. Artkey, founded in 1997, is the world's leading Asian art and licensing corporation. Owning exclusive rights to over 60,000 artworks by 700 Chinese artists, Artkey has catalyzed a whole movement of art appearing on everyday objects—handbags, watches, teacups, placemats, home décor, apparel, and stationery, as well as digital products such as screensavers, MMS, e-cards, wallpapers, and flash animation. As China looks to take its competitive advantage to the next level, enabled by government policy support and changes in design education, in-house design teams such as Lenovo's and independent design firms such as s.point and mooma will only have a bigger role to play in innovating with design. It is a long-term growth strategy that should have traditional design powerhouses such as Italy worried.

Think Chinese fashion and the names that usually spring to mind are Vivienne Tam, Jimmy Choo, and Shanghai Tang. These three brands have come to symbolize a Western interpretation of Chinese style—which David Tang maintains is "modernized Chinese, not East meets West," and Vivienne Tam proclaims as "design that melds the aesthetic and feminine mystique of Asia with the spirit of the modern world."[5] While these brands might have put cheongsams and Mandarin-collared shirts on the shelves of boutiques in Paris and New York, and *Sex and the City* has made Jimmy Choo's stilettos such objects of desire, most young people in China give these brands a miss, even as they stock up on Dior, Prada, and Chanel if they are super-rich, and H&M, Zara, and Mango if they are not. As Walter Ma, a fashion designer based in Hong Kong, says: "If you're Chinese, you don't have to say it with loud dragons." Which is what Vivienne Tam does—a dragon is exactly what you encounter as you launch her website.

Wang Wei is different. "I don't want to judge other Chinese fashion designers, but I do believe that redness and embroidered dragons aren't the only signature characteristics of Chinese fashion." [6] Showcased by the *Washington Post* in its article on innovation in China, the 34-year-old designer was the first native Chinese designer to exhibit at London Fashion Week, in 2006. His clothes do reflect a deconstructionist Chinese philosophy, but are aesthetically more Victoria & Albert Museum. His striking asymmetrical jackets and voluminous skirts are being noticed by fashion critics and magazines, and *Vogue* and *Elle* magazines feature his styles regularly.

Wang Wei's journey to the catwalks of London is one of absorbing Chinese influences, and then breaking away from them. Art was in Wang Wei's genes—his father was an artist, and he showed early signs of an aptitude for painting, representing Shanghai in art competitions by the time he was 13. He graduated in art from Donghua University in 1996, and switched to fashion design, propelled by the application of his art. "We Shanghainese tend to consider the commercial side of things," he says, explaining his move. His first job was in Hong Kong, where he worked for S.B. Polo, learning about how an international company functions and how it marketed its clothes. Chen Yifei—the painter-turned-fashion mogul—spotted him and recruited him to launch the Layefe brand. In building the brand, Wang Wei believed that rather than being self-absorbed, his design philosophy and style had to be presented to the world. In 2003, he created his own eponymous label, and moved to Europe to try and make a name for himself and his creations among the world's best. "Modern fashion is based on Western culture. You need to understand Western style and then inject your own philosophy in order to be successful,"[7] says Wang. While the seeds of change are indeed been sown in design education as Chinese design schools set up international exchange programs, Wang advises young students to "go outside for education—London, Paris, anywhere." His efforts are beginning to bear fruit. Following his landmark show in London, Wang was honored as one of the three Best Fresh Young Designers of the Year at the Paris trade show, *Who's Next.*

Jenny Ji has trod the path that Wang Wei recommends. But before she embarked on it, she had to take the conventional route. We met her one afternoon at her studio, which is right across the street from our office in Shanghai. Stepping out of her bright yellow Mercedes SLK 500, she looked every inch the successful entrepreneur

Fashion designer Jenny Ji
(Photo Courtesy of Jenny Ji)

to which the creative environment in China is giving birth. "I studied economics. Even though I liked painting when I was in school, I wasn't encouraged to follow it. People thought if one chose art, that was because you didn't get good scores at school. My parents said I would find it difficult to find a job. But in college, I didn't really like economics. I thought it was very boring, so I applied to some schools in Paris and Milan in my final year. I was accepted in both places, and chose to go to Milan to study fashion design."

The environment for pursuing an education and a subsequent career in the creative business has since changed. "Now, when you read newspapers, magazines—you read about lots of designers. You realize that it is one kind of job where you can be successful. Now, I have a cousin who says she too wants to do fashion design. It's a big change," she adds.

In Milan, Jenny suddenly came in contact with the world's top designers. "We saw their creations, touched them. It was a different feeling," she reminisces. Her class comprised students from the United States, Japan, Africa, even Nepal. It was a multicultural learning environment, and each student brought an instinctive cultural interpretation to his or her creation. Her stint in Milan also showed her how to break away from convention.

Jenny Ji's spring, summer 2008 collection and design studio
(Photos Courtesy of Jenny Ji)

Picking up a short, sexy dress from the clothes rack in her studio, she explained: "This is my interpretation of a *qipao*. Now, people say it's not a *qipao*—because it is white in color, and a *qipao* is supposed to be red, or some other bright color. I've made it sexy by shortening the length, so you can wear it with jeans. So my design is Western, but it has some Chinese elements." Then she showed us another piece. It was a military-style jacket, but not quite so; it was embroidered with beads, and was shiny. "My parents always wore the uniform. I took the basic design, changed the shape, added beads and made it more feminine." Jenny's other outfits have military stars and peony flowers embroidered or sequined on very Western outfits, such as jeans. "These are memories from my childhood. I've made them even more childish and colorful to accentuate their design," she says. Her designs are flying off the shelves. Jenny runs two boutiques—rubbing shoulders with Ermenegildo Zegna and Cartier at the swish M on the Bund, and the artsy Taikang Lu—and retails her clothes under two labels, La Vie and Jenny Ji. "Sixty percent of my customers are foreigners, but 40% are bought by mainland Chinese," she tells us. One of the mainlanders is so besotted with Jenny's designs that she has bought one piece of everything that she has ever designed.

Indeed, globalization has helped spread fashion literacy far and wide, both among the creators and the buyers. "These days, someone in Shanghai will be as in-the-know as someone in Milan," says Amanda Hallay, a fashion forecaster with the Donegar Group. There is a growing recognition that unexpected, new designs are emerging out of China. *Newsweek* magazine featured Jenny Ji in an article titled "Beyond Paris and Milan,"[8] remarking that cutting-edge designers are emerging in unexpected places. Shanghai is one of them. The government recently introduced a local Fashion Week in an effort to promote local labels and attract designers from abroad. Chanel held its fashion show at the Pudong International Airport in 2006; visitors were transported by a Chanel-emblazoned maglev train from the city center. Taxis in Shanghai showed videos of the backstage parties from Fashion Week, and there was a real sense of a fashion city coming through.

Plunging headlong into this fashion scene is 30-year-old designer He Yan. The quirky native of Jiangxi doesn't yet retail her clothes, selling mainly through personal contacts, and admits to being unable to send her parents any money at this stage. But when she launched her Malanhua collection in 2005, the fashionistas noticed. "There is no need to emphasize Chineseness," she said. "You're a Chinese, that's enough. If you purposefully boost yourself to be a Chinese, you'll create stuff that's too superficial."

Fashion designer He Yan

He Yan's 2006 collection, *Nue Xing*, has a distinct metrosexual feel—featuring a white jacket emblazoned with a bold orange floral motif, combined with low-slung shorts. Her inspiration—traditional Peking opera—is evident only in the strict attention to detail and seamless cuts. The metrosexuality comes from Japanese kabuki theater, where men play the female roles. In her designs for women, she turned to the suspender skirt that schoolgirls wore in the 1970s and 1980s. She retained the essence of the suspender, but added pocket details, which made the design slightly masculine. It was a look that she felt would be more appropriate for mature, confident, and independent girls.

"My inspiration comes from life as well as my personal feelings. I listen to songs, glance at overseas fashions, and surf the Internet. I don't think that creativity must be entirely original. I doubt that many designers can be completely original—we're always learning from others. You can recognize a Wang Yiyang creation at first sight, but some people say he's learning from the Japanese designer Rei Kawakuba. So you see how difficult it is to be original." The need for fashion to be practical isn't lost on He Yan. "As a designer, I care about what others feel when they wear my clothes. But it's not just about looking beautiful; it's about feeling comfortable as well,"[9] she says. Her efforts are paying off. In 2008, her clothes will be part of the "China Fashion" exhibition at the Victoria & Albert Museum in London.

Lu Kun is already being called the "John Galliano of China." His style is hard to define because a dizzying variety of elements can be found in his collection, from Chinese traditional details to Western flourishes. His autumn/winter collection in 2006 was inspired by the style of three powerful, legendary women: the perfect, goddess-like Evita Peron of Argentina; the eternally feminine former prime minister of Ukraine, Yulia Timoshenko; and the blue suits of Britain's "Iron Lady," Margaret Thatcher. The fashion sense of these women, as they held their own in a male-dominated political world, was reflected in the trousers Lu showcased on the catwalk. The only seeming concession to his Chinese origin showed in the use of tapestry satin material—"oriental mystery," as *Vogue China* called it.[10]

Vogue has also featured designer Ling Yali's work. Yali's avant-garde denim-inspired designs were the talk of the 2006 Shanghai Fashion Week, as she turned denim into dragon's paws, flower petals, wings, and swimming fish, and created evening dresses in exaggerated, multi-layered flounces. Her products had an unexpectedly strong touch of the surreal.

Not all designers are queuing up for the catwalks of Paris and Milan, though. Some are designing new fashion simply because they want to have fun or to do something different. Si Qi and Jin Ningning, both 27, met on the Internet, hit it off, and gave up their jobs to start their own studio, Perk. Nestled among the villas in Shanghai's French Concession, their shop doesn't even have a signboard, just a bright red door. The sky-blue interior and a rotating disco light above the cash counter gives some indication that their collection is quirky, colorful, and inspired by their emotions. Their merchandise features flying fairies, smiling watermelons, and funky images of plants and animals, all in bright colors. Unlike other designers, Qi and Ningning don't follow the norm of having spring/summer and autumn/winter collections, coming up with new designs only when they feel inspired. It's almost anti-market in some ways, but in their inimitable style, they represent a growing sentiment among designers not to be dictated to by the market. "We don't really care about what other designers are doing. We just make our own stuff," says Jin. As much as their pieces are unique—only three of a particular jacket may be made—they also like to make their fashion accessible to the young. A pair of slacks retails at RMB380 (around US$50), a T-shirt at RMB180 (US$24). At the Young Designer's Showcase in Shanghai's Xintiandi, Perk's show was inspired by children enjoying the circus. Against a backdrop of fairground music, models sashayed in costumes that were a mismatch of patterns and polka dots, sometimes wearing checked bowler hats with two-piece suits, sometimes dangling toys in their hands. Shirts were laced with sequins, pants were made from PVC—all in shocking candy colors. In more ways than one, it was—like the Perk label itself—designed to overcome boredom.

In spite of the recent excitement surrounding haute couture and prêt-a-porter, the fashion design scene in China remains both challenging and promising. It is challenging because the market is flooded with international offers at all price points. With their ever-rising incomes, consumers are often looking for the international label to flash. Lu Kun says, "[Fashion design] students need to be aware that as they advance in their careers, competition will get tougher and customers will expect more and more. They need to look to the big brands, not as a source of inspiration, but as competition, and should focus on their own strengths to create strategic advantage." It is promising because of the ever-growing levels of fashion consciousness. In a 2005 study commissioned by *Vogue China*, and conducted by the Huakun Women's Life Survey Center in eight major cities, 32.3% of the women surveyed thought of themselves as very fashionable; 47.6% said they would follow fashion if they could afford it; and 35.7% thought that to be fashionable, the most remarkable characteristic should be "different style and personality"[11]—a clear indication of their quest for individuality. In our own study conducted among consumers in the lower-tier cities in China, we found that the craving to be up to date with fashion was slightly higher in the third-tier cities—37.7%— than in the first-tier cities, where it was 35.8%.

Be it local brands or international ones, it is evident that from the point of view of the fashion customer, there are ever more opportunities to wear creativity on their shoulders, to flaunt it wherever they go. As people seek to define their identity through fashion, they are constantly experimenting and being ever more creative with their choices. The greater sense of style that the product and fashion designers are generating among people is sure to play out in what consumers expect their chosen brands to say about them.

---

[1] Dexter Roberts, "A Legend for How Long?" *BusinessWeek*, May 15, 2000.

[2] www.lenovoblogs.com/designmatters/.

[3] *s.point design: Designing Tomorrow—Case Studies of Product Design in China* (Tsinghua University, 2006).

[4] www.newmoma.com/E/aboutus.htm.

[5] www.viviennetam.com.

[6] www.chinadaily.com.cn/cndy/2007-04/27/content_861284.htm.

[7] Amy Fabris-Shi, "Journey to the West—Designer Wang Wei's Quest for Success," *That's Shanghai*, July 2007.

[8] *Newsweek International*, July 2–9, 2007.

[9] Apple Mandy, "In Bloom—He Yan Introduces Her New Collection," *That's Shanghai*, August 2006.

[10] *Vogue China*, September 2006, p. 140.

[11] www.womenofchina.cn/research/statistics/9809.jsp.

Stimulant of the Masses
The creative phenomenon that is sweeping the nation

"Creativity is about something that is valuable and allows us to experience life afresh. It can turn the useless into useful, save space and energy, lighten up life, and make it more colorful. With creativity, things are more comfortable, more interesting, and more fun."

Lian Qingguang, 26 , IT engineer, Zhongshan

Personalized T-shirt shop at Nanjing's Fashion Lady marketplace

Many of the examples that I have given in the previous chapters are suggestive of individual will and ability, enabled by a new environment that encourages innovation in China. The question that begs answering is: Is this creativity a mass movement? Or is the phenomenon confined to a few? It was in search of everyday, commonplace creativity that my colleagues and I embarked on a journey through the streets of China, into the marketplaces and people's homes.

As we immersed ourselves, we found that ordinary people were using creativity to break through monotony and stereotypes. In people's homes, and on the streets, we found they were being driven by the practical applications of creativity; some were using it to save money or to enhance their competitiveness and earn profit. They were being inspired by the challenges that life itself was throwing at them, and by people around them, and quite often, finding a creative solution to problems required hard work. It wasn't about a light bulb coming on while in the shower at all. Let me describe what we saw.

In spite of the soaring growth in China's automobile industry —a 30% year-on-year increase in the sales of passenger cars in 2007—it is still quite common to find many people riding bicycles, motorcycles, and motor scooters on the streets of Chinese cities. They not only have to deal with the chaotic traffic, but also with the extreme weather conditions and pollution. Come summer, almost every woman riding a two-wheeler dons a sheer white cotton over-garment, a cross between a poncho and a shawl worn over her dress, and snaps on a sun-visor. Obsessed with staying fair-skinned, these "sunscreens" help prevent tanning of the face and arms and provide some physical protection from the glare and grit. Check out the local market, and it seems that the bicycle accessory market is booming. Shops sell sun-visors by the dozen, and the cotton ponchos are available in many styles, with and without lace trim. When the temperature drops to freezing and below in winter, many two-wheeler riders cope with the problem of freezing hands by attaching to the handles of their bike a cheap leather or PVC tube, into which they slide

Improvization with shades and shawls

The slide-in, keep-warm rubber tube

their hands to keep them warm as they ride.

Protection against the elements is also sought by trishaw drivers across the nation. In Beijing, the trishaws that offer tours of the city's historic narrow streets and alleys (*hutongs*) are equipped with bright red covers to protect against the sun or rain; while in Guangzhou, Shanghai, and other cities, the drivers make improvised covers from bamboo or pieces of PVC sheeting from old billboards. These are creative solutions to practical problems.

Take another situation. Cruises on the Yangtze River are popular among the wealthy and the upper-middle class. The cruise ships, however, traverse some of the more economically depressed regions of China. Children from impoverished families often line the riverbank, begging for alms. But because the river is deep in places and the current strong, they attach small bags to long bamboo poles, which they thrust toward the decks of the passing ships. A lot of renminbi is collected in this creative manner.

"Creativity comes when you are in a difficult situation," said a group of young men we spoke with in Wuxi, in Jiangsu province. "When you are under pressure, you just have to think about the problem from a different angle, and come up with a solution." It is life itself that provides the masses with creative inspiration, and that is not very different from what inspires the "creative people," as we define them.

One problem that many Chinese have yet to overcome is the problem of limited cash resources. Making their money go further, often through recycling, becomes a key driver for them to think creatively. Gao Qi, a 33-year-old Beijing engineer, glued together the pieces of a broken vase and drilled holes into which he inserted plastic flowers. "This new vase is even more beautiful than the one that broke," he said, proud of his creativity and craftsmanship. In Guangzhou, we saw a no–parking sign attached to a broken chair; rather than discard it, the shop owner used it as a frame for his sign and put it on the pavement in front of his shop. Another used old plumbing to create some striking signage for his apparel shop. A homeowner in Wuxi embedded broken porcelain pieces in a circular pattern at the entrance to his home, to make an interesting anti-skid surface. A fruit-seller in Beijing affixed the canopy of an old umbrella to a bamboo pole, to make a sunshade for herself. Farmers in Dali, in Yunnan province, have found an interesting use for their empty sacks of fertilizer and grain: transporting chickens. They poke holes in the sacks, place the chickens inside with their heads sticking out, and then stash the sacks on the backs of their pickup trucks, or even on the bicycle carrier, for transportation. The birds stay quiet, remain still, and seem to like the swaddling; and the farmer doesn't have to buy any cages.

A broken chair makes a no-parking sign

Broken porcelain makes an anti-skid surface

The functional value of creativity that such examples illustrate is carried forward in other forms. An "outsider" in China, one of the first things I noticed on the streets was that babies wore pants that seemed to be ripped at the back. But when I saw a mother changing her baby's diaper in double-quick time, I realized the utility of the "product feature." In the back lanes of Nanjing, one of my colleagues pointed out a lock on a water faucet. Evidently, not everyone in the neighborhood had a water connection. This family had found a creative way to prevent others stealing its water.

An umbrella attached to a bicycle handlebar

Traditional crafts-candy sticks on sale in Chengdu

Ni Kai, a 25-year-old bank clerk in Wuxi, showed us some toy spiders he had fashioned out of discarded electrical wires. "I like changing the useless into the useful," he said. The usual instinct for most people would be to throw away the chopsticks that come with takeaway noodle meals. Not so for Gu Hongmin, a manager in a state-owned enterprise, also in Wuxi. She washes used chopsticks and uses them to create pen stands. Gu Jin, in Nanjing, had pasted empty cola bottle caps on a piece of board in a pattern such that it formed a large cola bottle. On a much grander scale, the art districts of Dashanzi and Moganshan, in Beijing and Shanghai, respectively, have recycled existing spaces for new uses; the studio-owners haven't had to spend any money on building the basic structures.

It is these unusual uses of everyday things that can be termed "creative." So, how do these people get their ideas? Are they born creative, or is it a sense they acquire? "You have to be observant. Go out to different places. Maybe you'll spot something simple that you haven't thought of before, and that could spark off an idea. No observation ability means no inspiration," said a group of women in Wuxi.

An important function that creativity serves common people is to help them make their lives more organized. Many living environments in China are small and cluttered. When Zhang Haitao, a 35-year-old IT professional in Zhongshan, creates a stand out of corrugated board in which to store his compact discs, and when Zhu Ying, a 27-year-old government official in Wuxi, nails a couple of tube-like potato-chip containers on her bathroom wall in which to store wet umbrellas, they are trying to organize things in their homes; their creativity is unwitting. A 22-year-old student in Beijing combined his recycling and space-optimization instincts and created a bookshelf for his dorm room from discarded planks of wood and empty beer bottles. Indeed, one of the favorite look-in places for many young couples in Beijing, Shanghai, and Guangzhou is the 35-square-meter show flat in their local Ikea store. The design optimizes every square centimeter of space, organizing living and storage areas both aesthetically and cost-effectively. Several of the respondents in our focus groups brought along objects or cuttings from the Ikea catalogue to demonstrate what they thought were great ideas for organizing their living spaces better: clothes hangers that could hang more than one pair of trousers; the remote control organizer that can be hung on the sofa armrest; a stool with space to store magazines. "Creativity is about someone or something going beyond what is expected," said the group in Wuxi.

On many occasions, we found it was the sheer pleasure of adding beauty to their lives that made people's creative instinct come alive. Along with the sense of accomplishment they derived from their endeavors, they reveled in the appreciation that they earned from their friends, family, and colleagues. Ma Junwei, a nurse in Wuxi, makes interesting gift bouquets. "I use chocolates instead of flowers. The flavors of the chocolates can vary, depending on the person the bouquet is intended for." Zhang Yuesong, a 30-year-old administrative officer in Beijing, and his wife used beads to make a box for holding tissues. Evidently not one to limit his creativity to tissue boxes, he also created an ikebana display using, instead of flowers, vegetables such as baby tomatoes, lettuce, and asparagus for his wife on Valentine's Day. "She was amused and

A bouquet of teddy bears

loved it so much," he said, laughing. Florists in the marketplace are quick to turn these individual acts into a new "product range." On Valentine's Day in 2007, one of the hottest-selling items was a bouquet made with small teddy bears. The fact that the soft toys wouldn't wither after a couple of days seemed appropriately emblematic of the duration of the romance. On the banks of the Yellow River in Lanzhou, we observed young couples painting figurines of comic characters together. Some of it was evidently about giving Hello Kitty and Dora a personal interpretation. For the less artistically accomplished, yet both creatively and romantically inclined, little shops in Nanjing's underground Fashion Lady market offer to paint portraits of your loved ones, surrounded by little hearts, on T-shirts.

There are others who are imbuing everyday objects with beauty. He Weidong, a 23-year-old salesman, likes collecting stones, painting designs on them, and arranging them in his home. Yang Qianxi, a 25-year-old teacher in Chengdu, draws lovely pictures on eggshells and stones, which he gives to his friends. Zhang Weichuan, a

Personalized T-shirt at Nanjing's Fashion Lady marketplace

29-year-old sales director in Zhongshan, had an innovative idea when he was decorating his new home. He made a hole in the wall of the living room, into which he placed an aquarium. It saved space, looked good, and was practical: "Because the washroom is on the other side, it makes changing the water much more convenient." Tian Guo, a 27-year-old housewife in Chengdu, was flush with self-achievement as she refurbished her home. "I participated in the whole process of decorating my apartment. It is my design. I didn't save much more than my friends, but the overall effect is much better. I feel good." Hu Ke, a 26-year-old engineer in Chengdu, made a clothes bin using his wife's leftover Hello Kitty wallpaper. It was bright, cheerful, and unique. The previously mentioned Zhang Haitao, from Zhongshan, uses disposable paper plates to make photo frames. Such DIY is on

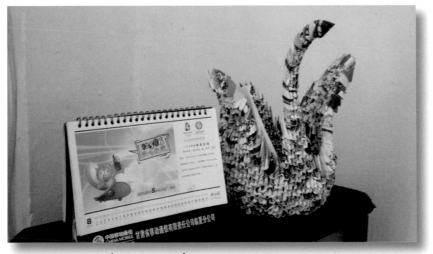

A paper swan made by a housewife in Linxia, Gansu province

the rise, and businesses—big and small—are beginning to recognize the trend. Little shops in markets such as Yu Yuan in Shanghai and Fashion Lady in Nanjing hawk appliqué hearts and stars, beads, and ribbons to sew on jeans and skirts. adidas has introduced an "adicolor" range of white shoes, which come in a box with paint tubes the buyer can use to create his or her own designs.

This urge to turn the commonplace into objects of appreciation and admiration has resulted in a new business opportunity right across China—the professional portfolio studio. From early childhood—the moment the baby starts resembling anything like a cherub—to the fairytale wedding, creating photo albums and posters is now a national obsession. Integral to the photo shoot is styling—and the photographer's entourage comprises makeup artists and location designers. Couples pose in tuxedos and wedding gowns in front of a church, in a garden, on boats, where they may be depicted pouring rose petals on their lover's back. They then shift gears to a more traditional look, as they don *qipaos* and traditional men's costumes and cavort among the stone forests and carved wooden pavilions in locations such as the Temple of Heaven and Suzhou Gardens. A similar pattern is followed with children, with large stuffed toys being a *de rigueur* accessory. In one more unusual case, I saw a child being turned into a pint-size commando wielding a toy submachine gun. The final product of this creative endeavor is usually a bound photo album and a set of oversize prints to be framed and hung in the home. It is all a wonderful fantasy that is being played out, and one from which the new creative entrepreneurs are profiting.

Portfolio mania: wedding album shoot in progress

Page from a child's photo album, Lanzhou

As more such photo studios emerge, the pressure to do something different increases. We chanced upon one studio that specialized in shooting nude portfolios of young women who aspire to be models, or film and television stars.

On the streets, China is awash with people who make a living out of craft and their creative skills. At almost every popular tourist destination, visitors are likely to be accosted by artists who sit them down and quickly sketch their portrait for the equivalent of a couple of dollars. On my way to the

Mask-like figures on sale in Chengdu

Old wire artist, French
Concession, Shanghai

Confucius Temple in Beijing, one such artist walked with me and painted my likeness on a small porcelain plate, which I felt compelled to buy. In Shanghai's French Concession, an old man sits on the pavement, under the shade of a plane tree, and fashions trishaws, bicycles, dragons, and animals out of pieces of wire. (Wu Yifan uses the same materials, but creates fascinating Japanese manga characters, which he sells through a boutique for RMB100 [around US$13]. He obviously has the smarter business model.) In a busy marketplace in Guangzhou, we spotted two women, aged in their sixties, making colorful six-inch-tall dolls out of wool, which they sold for RMB20 (less than US$3).

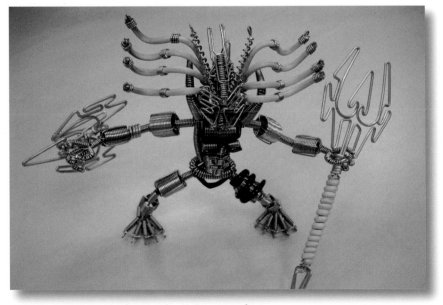

Manga-inspired wire figure, made by Wu Yifan

Wu Yifan and his manga-inspired wire masterpieces

Some people we spoke with considered humor and happiness to be key ingredients of creativity. "It should be about expressing or capturing the lighter side of life. Creativity makes life colorful, no longer boring; it brings delight in an otherwise routine or depressed life," said a group of young men in Zhongshan. The way they took digs at each other and used objects like their mobile phones were also manifestations of their creativity. One explained that he always arranges on a napkin the bones from his takeaway fried chicken meal to resemble the human body, using the Colonel's face as the head of the figure. One strategy commonly used to create humor is to juxtapose things in an unexpected way. For instance, the extremely popular song by Yang Chengang, "*Lao Shu Ai Da Mi,*" which literally translates as "I Love You Like Mice Love Rice," breaks away from the routine expressions of love, such as evoking the smell of flowers or the sight of the sea. The lip-syncing of the Backdorm Boys and the parodies of Hu Ge are great examples of creativity by ordinary people. Many of the people we talked with referred to text-messaging and online chats (and the use of emoticons) as humorous creativity being played out in everyday life. The latest fad to hit the screens in China is Tuzkism, based on a simple, expressive rabbit character called Tuzki created by Wang Momo, a student at the Beijing Broadcasting Institute.

What was common among most of the people we spoke with or visited was that they didn't fit the conventional definition of "creative" or "artistic" people. Neither were they young teenagers who embrace creativity as a way of adopting and projecting an identity. These were engineers, accountants, nurses, teachers, and government officials, yet they were practicing some form of creativity or another. In most cases, they undervalued their own creativity. "We just find solutions to everyday problems. What we have are little smart ideas. That's dealing with life." Truly creative people, they felt, "always come up with ideas—it is regular behavior for them." Their true measure of creativity would be in terms of an idea having a big impact on the people around them, or even on society as a whole. In other cases, the recognition they got from the people around them—spouses, colleagues, friends, and relatives—provided them with a sense of accomplishment and superiority. "After I had finished doing up my home, I couldn't wait to show it to my friends," Tian Guo told us. And Zhang Xuesong commented: "Because of my creative ideas, I can do things others can't."

There are others who are being recognized as much for their creative abilities as for their efforts in preserving traditional Chinese cultural history. Kite-making is one element of that history, and a fertile ground for a mass exposition of creativity, as the colorful shapes take flight in public spaces—Beijing's Tiananmen-Square being one of them. In ancient China, the kite was known as a *zhiyuan* or paper glider. Originally regarded as an item of technology, the kite also featured prominently in many art collections, and was considered to have unique artistic value. It first appeared in the wars of the Spring and Autumn Period (770–476 BC). The master carpenter Lu Ban made kites which were flown high to spy on the enemy. During the famous Chu-Han War of 206–202 BC, the general of the Han troops, Zhang Liang, ordered his soldiers to fly kites in the heavy fog around the Chu troops who were being led by Xiang Yu. Children sitting on the large kites played tunes from Chu (the present Hubei province) on flutes. Hearing the melodies, the Chu soldiers began missing their homes and scattered without a fight. Kites were also used during this period to deliver urgent messages. The role of the kite evolved during the prosperous Tang dynasty. Making and flying various kites reflected the pleasant mood of springtime, and the tradition of flying kites as a leisure activity has endured. Kites come in all sizes and shapes—dragonfly, swallow, centipede, butterfly, insects, goldfish, clouds. Swallow-shaped kites are quite popular in Beijing. Craftsmen fashion them in many different ways. Some are strewn with peonies, bats, and other auspicious patterns to bring the owner good fortune. Kites made in Nantong usually come complete with whistles and bells. When airborne, they resemble a formation of birds. A kite made in Tianjin is in the form of a swallow, with dozens of little "swallows" attached.

Kite-maker Lv TieZhi

Lv Tiezhi is considered one of the foremost exponents of kite-making in China today. He is one of the few surviving inheritors of the Jinma faction of the Beijing school of kite making, and became famous after Beijing TV aired a documentary about his work in 1996. In 1998, he was sent overseas by the government to promote the craft. In 2000, the US government granted him the title "Master of Kite Art." Experimentation characterizes Lv Tiezhi's work. "My master, Guan Baoxiang, told me: 'You don't have to learn all the details from me. What you should do is learn the spirit of kite art. You shouldn't follow all the traditions—rather, you should develop them and give them a new life.' So, I've been keeping my mind open and learning from other arts." He showed us one of his works. "This is a kite I designed for the BMW company. I used the typical swallow figure for BMW, and embodied the logo into the swallow's eyes and belly. The client just loved it and it is now in their collection," he said. Lv Tiezhi feels that evolution is an inevitable characteristic of creativity. "It is about making progress," he stressed.

Dough sculpture, a traditional folk art in China, dates back to the Han dynasty (206 BC–AD 219) and is representative of the creative use of everyday materials. People used dough to make colorful figurines and decorations for special occasions—birthdays, weddings, and even as sacrificial offerings. In Shaanxi province, there is a mass creative expression every year, when hundreds of people make exquisite sculptures as offerings to the local deity at the Lancheng Temple. These offerings symbolize the pursuit of truth, kindness, and beauty. Lang Shaoan was born in 1909 to a Manchurian family in Beijing. When he was 13, he met a man making dough figures at a spring festival fair. He was so fascinated by the vivid works that he asked to become the man's student. For the next 70 years, Lang's work brought even greater fame to dough sculpture, earning him the name "Dough Figurine Lang." Most of his sculptures were inspired by the heroes and heroines of Peking opera. Some depicted historical tales or images of everyday life. When Lang makes his figurines, he improves the dough, mixing in a little glutinous rice flour to enhance its stickiness; he uses honey to prevent the figurines from breaking when dry. The pigments used in the dough are carefully selected, so that the colors of the figurines don't fade over time. The craft is passed down through the generations. Lang Zhichun, his son, has inherited his father's techniques and then passed this folk art to the third generation—his 10-year-old son, Lang Jiaziyu.

Zhang Bolin is a member of the Folk Art Association of Wuxi, and is considered one of the foremost innovators of the craft. His contribution lies in the depiction of Chinese epics such as *Eight Immortals Crossing the Sea* and *Journey to the West* through his dough figurines. He is invited to many cities for live shows, and many newspapers carry his story. "Creativity should keep pace with changes in society. Even as we learn traditional crafts and depict traditional stories, we have to bring in modern themes—otherwise you will be eliminated," he says. Eggshell painter Tao Rong agrees.

Dough artist Zhang Bolin

"Based on my experience, most of the Chinese folk arts that people buy are not purely traditional. You have to be connected to the market; only then will you have prospects for doing good business," she says. She believes that creativity is about "doing something that others haven't done yet. It makes your audience excited," the Chengdu-born artist says. Her works—eggs painted with colorful landscapes, vivid characters, and bright flowers—sell not only in China, but also in Spain, the United States, and Japan.

Crosstalk (*xiangsheng* in Chinese; literally, "face and voice") is a traditional form of comic dialogue that dates from China's imperial Qing dynasty (1644–1911). Usually performed by two people, it can also be performed by one person or even a group of people. The performers try their best to make fun of, or to take advantage of, the other(s) through skillful play on words, a technique that brings to the fore the craft and wit of the Chinese language. In the old days in Tianjin, Beijing, and elsewhere, crosstalkers performed at temple fairs and street markets. More famous performers were invited to perform in teahouses and theaters. Crosstalk pieces draw on every aspect of Chinese culture, from history and folk tales to contemporary social issues. Although there are hundreds of pieces in the traditional repertoire, they are usually edited to suit the times and the audience.

The traditional performance art of crosstalk is making a comeback with the help of crosstalk specialist Guo Degang. Guo arrived in Beijing from Tianjin in 1995 to embark on his crosstalk career, only to find that the art form was on the decline. In 1995, Guo chanced upon a teahouse where he found several young people performing crosstalk. Being a crosstalker himself, he couldn't resist taking to the stage. Gradually, more and more people came to the teahouse to see him perform. He soon found himself playing to more than 100 people in a teahouse that could accommodate only 80.

As his popularity grew, Guo pondered the future of his art. "Traditional crosstalk is at least half an hour long, but performances are no longer than five minutes on TV, which kills much of the story. TV is part of the fast-food culture and crosstalk is a face-to-face art form—it needs interaction, and isn't suited to TV," Guo said. He was determined to bring the art form back to its roots. In 1996, Guo and some young crosstalk actors founded the Deyun Crosstalk Association, with the aim of returning crosstalk to teahouses and theaters. Over the next 10 years, the association organized countless performances in teahouses across Beijing. Despite their growing popularity, Guo ensured that ticket prices were kept low to make the art form accessible to everyone. Guo doesn't belong to an official group or troupe, and has never performed on TV. But attending his crosstalk performance is becoming increasingly trendy in Beijing, especially for young executives, and schoolchildren who load their MP3 players with his works. He might not be mainstream, but Guo is able to command 25 encores that can add some three hours to his originally scheduled two-hour performance.[1]

In January 2006, Guo was invited to perform at the People's Liberation Army Opera House in Beijing. Although the performance wasn't formally advertised, many fans turned up and jammed the box office trying to get tickets. Tickets were sold for RMB20 (US$2.70) but had a black market value of as much as RMB300 (US$40). Traditional performance art had found its market.

Undoubtedly, it wouldn't be possible for many of these creative artists to survive without government support in the initial stages. But as they discover a market—comprising both native Chinese and foreigners—that is appreciative of their craft and values it in monetary terms, they are imbuing the culture with a sense of aesthetics that compels us to look at the everyday in a new light.

As China hurtles along its chosen path toward modernization, its young people are on a search for their identity. They use creativity to express a range of possible identities—perhaps not yet as extreme as the schoolgirls of Tokyo's Shibuya district, but surely inspired by it. In the past couple of years, Japan's Cosplay (a contraction of two words, costume and play) phenomenon, where people dress as characters out of *manga* comics and video games, is gaining popularity in China in a remarkable manner. The interplay between the government's desire to control the influences on its people and the people's own desires is a remarkable tale of how the masses can use creativity to determine and define their own identities.

A Cosplayer plays a character from a Korean comic book

A Cosplayer struts her stuff at the   Becoming a fairy
Shanghai Animation Festival

Animation and cartoons were popular in China in the 1950s and 1960s. However, they usually told dull tales of good children helping people, in the spirit of Chairman Mao. With the opening-up era of the 1980s, a spate of foreign cartoons—such as *Astro Boy* and *Transformers* from Japan, and popular Disney shows—caught the imagination of young people. Along with smuggled Japanese and Taiwanese comic books, they sent the local cartoon industry into a creative recession. China's child and teen population today stands at 370 million, and it represents a huge animation market, occupied mostly by Japanese, American, Taiwanese, and South Korean producers. Concerned about these imports, and its content—usually viewed as a violent counterculture devoid of any positive social message, the government established the China National Centre for Developing the Animation, Cartoon and Game Industry under the Ministry of Culture. The center was entrusted with the task of regulating content, as well as boosting the status of the domestic animation industry. Hangzhou, in Zhejiang province, was chosen as the hub for the industry. At the International Cartoon and Animation

Festival held in the city in June 2007, officials seated beneath a row of inflatable cartoon animals lauded the role of animation in "socialist development" and promoted cartoons that, while based on traditional Chinese stories, are created using fashionable modern animation techniques.

The young Cosplayers aren't buying any of it. Outside, two men dressed in leather costumes and with white spiky hair brandished giant swords and fought for the affections of a young woman wearing a yellow wig and a miniskirt. As Japanese rock music blared in the background, a horde of fans, many wearing bright wigs and Mickey Mouse ears, applauded. These young men and women, many just out of school, call themselves *Xinxin Renlei* (New New Human Beings). They are young and independent, sensitive to individual choice and freedom, act spontaneously, embrace risk and adventure, and are ready to challenge established rules and morality. They exhibit the classic traits of a creative culture, and are inspired by the imagery that contemporary international media throws at them. Cosplay allows them to experiment with their identity. Fei Fei, a 19-year-old student wearing a kimono, says: "You can become someone else for a while, express things that you can't normally express yourself."[2]

The Cosplay phenomenon in China has been fanned by a clutch of animation, merchandise, and computer game companies who have held events in shopping malls in Shanghai, Suzhou, Hangzhou, Beijing, Xi'an, Liaoning, and Guangzhou. For a few years, the trend remained underground. Then, in August 2005, tom.com, a popular website that is home to popular forums for animation, *manga* comic, and computer game fans, held China's first Full Dress Carnival Animation Festival at Beijing's Military Museum. An explosion of websites, bulletin boards, and offline events followed, increasing the opportunities for young people to participate in the subculture.

Cao Fei is a new-generation artist whose work jumps from photography to DV to theater. Born in Guangzhou in 1978, she grew up in a world that was populated by Hong Kong pop, TV drama, computer games, *manga*, American rap, and Hong Kong kung fu cinema. Her film *Cosplayers* is a manifesto that challenges conventional notions: young people can no longer be confined to the limiting, "elitist" circle of the art world. In the film, the Cosplayers, cloaked in metallic suits and black capes, chase each other across fields near Guangzhou and stalk anonymous urban spaces, as the camera takes in the gigantic construction sites and herds of livestock in an attempt to grasp the contrasts in the heart of a modern city. For filmmakers like Cao, and animators struggling to find their place in a market dominated by international players, the recently established Shanghai Comic Party offers the opportunity to get together and be inspired, as well as to spot business opportunities. Held annually at the East Asia Exhibition Hall, the event features costume contests (not confined to Cosplay characters, but extending to the innocuous Dora and the omnipresent Mickey Mouse), film shows, comic author and artist signings, comic book stalls, and trade exhibits. When we visited the exhibition, it was packed with young people, and the show's organizers predict that it will soon assume the scale of the region's top animation event— Tokyo's Comiket, which draws more than 120,000 visitors.

The skyrocketing interest in and engagement with animation has the authorities looking at it from a new angle; no longer is it seen as a threatening subculture, but rather as a potential export industry. As Taiwanese and Hong Kong companies are increasingly using China as a base to create animation, and as they are being followed by Hollywood, the government has designated Hangzhou and other cities as "animation industry bases" and is beginning to pour in enormous sums of money. Half a billion dollars is being invested in Changzhou, in Jiangsu province, to build digital animation for online games. The number of universities now offering animation courses exceeds 400. Like many other things, it is a typical path: provide the environment, and things will follow. Only, in this case, it is not the ability to mass-manufacture that we're talking about; it is a surge of original creations. David Ehrlich, who teaches at the Beijing Film Academy, is optimistic about the future: "The issue is, can they make more original material? I think it can be done."[3]

Throughout our conversations with people from all walks of life in China, we asked them to define creativity. They identified four main characteristics.

First, it is about disrupting convention and breaking through stereotypes. In a society such as China where the political system and social order impose a set of rules and precepts about ideal behavior, and create stereotypical models that serve as examples of the ideal, many people feel the need to express themselves by breaking away from the norm. Creativity is about the unexpected, about breaking the monotony and routine of life itself.

Second, the practical and functional applications of creativity seem paramount. Without application, creativity loses its meaning. "Creativity has to be meaningful. If you create something that can't be used in the real world, it is just trash," said Yuan Ling, a 20-year-old student in Chengdu. Many of the common person's efforts are appreciated simply because they add some value in a practical sense, or they solve a problem in a very functional, but unexpected, manner. One of the expected functions of creativity is to enhance our quality of life. Through creativity, people can find greater economic or social value, which enhances their self-esteem and earns the admiration of others. "Great creativity can bring big profits," said Xe Hu, a 24-year-old investment consultant in Beijing. More and more people like him are putting their money behind ideas in the new Chinese economy.

Cane baby carrier, Chengdu

The third dimension, and an interesting one that once again challenges convention, is that creativity is the result of thinking very hard. It is not a sudden spark that you have; but rather the outcome of "industrious thinking," in the words of Xu Chen, a 32-year-old administrative officer. Creative people have to work just as hard; they have to look for what's new—which is tough by itself. They must then think about applications and the result, be it for themselves or for a larger society. "The creative process requires you to come up with many ideas or thoughts, and to throw away most of them," Gu Hongmin, from Wuxi, explained.

Many people we spoke with cited Deng Xiaoping as the most creative person China has seen in a long time. Not as an artist, a filmmaker, a musician, or an architect who made buildings—but as the architect of modern China. Deng's creativity embodied the three most important dimensions of creativity. His ideas about China's future trajectory and the embracing of a free market economy were antithetical to the established norms of communism. He didn't think of "opening up" as a mere slogan; it was backed up by reform, the search for markets, and the creation of new opportunities for all people. It was goal-oriented, not an ideology. And finally, Deng spent a long time thinking about his strategy, especially during the years he was out of favor. He had to think of ways he could counter his foes, of how to rally public support for his policies and convince them of the potential benefits.

The fourth dimension of creativity lies in the fact that it is inspired by life (a rubber tire as a basketball hoop). Life throws up many challenges and opportunities, and one only has to dig into one's memories to come up with ideas. "You have to be a life-observer," said Li Lu, a 22-year-old teacher in Beijing. "Observe not just your own life, but the lives of people around you." She evidently finds the activities of the children she teaches very inspiring.

After analyzing the experiences of the many creative people we met and have described in this and the preceding chapters, as well as the views of many ordinary people we spoke with, we have come to the conclusion that there are two primary facets of creativity:

- Creativity is equated with innovative capability, but it needs to be imbued with meaning and functionality—that is, it cannot be an abstract phenomenon or object.

- Creativity must satisfy a need, and it must be accepted by a majority; it cannot be the preserve of a few.

Therein lies the crucial difference between West and East in understanding creativity. Whereas in the West greater emphasis is placed on people's sense of humor and aesthetic taste, Chinese people tend to emphasize social influences, such as being inspirational to others and contributing to the progress of society.

Indeed, for contemporary China, *creativity is the reform that is driving social progress.* It is an imperative, a competitive advantage that can be nurtured and built as China seeks to evolve from a manufacturing economy to be a key player in the next level of the global knowledge economy, where cultural capital will count and creative ability will provide the means to negotiate.

The time is right. Will companies wake up to the challenge?

---

[1] Chen Lin, "The Return of Traditional Crosstalk," www.china.org.cn, February 3, 2006.

[2] Duncan Hewitt, "A State of Fantasy," *Newsweek International,* July 30, 2007.

[3] Ibid.

Revelation:
The Business Imperative
Busting some common myths about Chinese creativity

"With one foot firmly in the past, and the other stepping into the future, China is simultaneously the world's largest startup and turnaround."

James McGregor, *One Billion Customers*

Young creatives display their work at the iMart Festival

T raditionally, only people with certain traits were thought of as being "creative," while others without those traits were not. A creative personality is often assumed to be the basis for creative action. Characteristics such as independence, risk-taking behavior, and freedom from social conventions all make up the traits of such a personality. As our views of creativity have become more informed, we have come to appreciate the role of hard work and revision in the process. Many scholars as well as ordinary people recognize that creativity isn't always about extraordinary inventions; it is an incremental process that adds value to things or thinking that already exists. This thinking suggests that creativity need not be the preserve of a few, or the gifted. It can be imbibed, learned, and used by many to solve problems. The presence of adversity is a factor that often encourages people to use creativity. Creativity must also be relevant to one's culture at a given point in time. When we use expressions such as "an idea whose time has come," we refer to the value that the idea has gained at that point in time. This underlines the importance of context in judging the value of a creative idea. Finally, even as many believe that great inventors or artists are among the most creative people, what contemporary business organizations must recognize is that, in the words of the French mathematician and physicist Henri Poincaré, "ideas rise from the crowds." Creativity involves an associative form of thought, in which ideas float, collide, and eventually connect.

In the preceding chapters, I have laid out the evidence of China's emergence as a place where creativity can indeed flourish. But harnessing China's creative potential would involve some fundamental shifts in mindset by business enterprises. Here, I will challenge some of the assumptions that are commonly held about the place of creativity in Chinese society and business.

> **Myth 1:** Chinese people have yet to emerge from the ideological indoctrination of the mid-20th century, which compelled them to think, dress, and behave alike.

> **Reality:** A huge majority of people in China are finding ways of differentiating themselves.

One of the telling quotations that I came across before I arrived in China was: "It seems that the leaders have struck a deal with the people. 'You are free to make as much money as you can, as long as you don't interfere with politics.'" This doesn't remain as a mere belief; we see it practiced in everyday life. That the Chinese

Hand-painted sneakers,
a symbol of individuality,
on sale at the iMart Festival

people have embraced the rewards of capitalism without resorting to democracy is proof of their creative management of their polity. Those over the age of 40 have historically identified themselves with mainstream values; and the government slogans emphasize social order and harmony. The Beijing Olympics slogan, "One World, One Dream," is a very good example. But since the mid-1990s, the government has also allowed people to choose the jobs they want to do, as opposed to their being allocated jobs, mostly in state-owned enterprises (SOEs). This freedom was accompanied by a sense of competition and the need to differentiate oneself in order to get ahead. In the scenario where many had the same academic qualifications and work experience, the only way to find jobs in the market, now populated with local businesses and multinational corporations along with the SOEs, was through differentiation. Over the last decade, the sense of competition has only become keener, among people and in the marketplace. Projecting a unique identity—whether you are one shop among 15 others on a street selling the same products, or one of 50 applicants for a position—requires creativity.

In some instances, differentiation is cemented through a cultural identity that prevails over national identity. For example, many Shanghainese are very conscious of and concerned about protecting their local Shanghainese identity in a kind of reaction to the centrally imposed Putonghua. Many have started writing blogs in their own dialect, and some have even become well known for doing so. Most residents in the city are only second–or third–generation descendants of the people who moved to the city in the

1950s. So the dialect has been influenced by the other dialects from surrounding areas, including Ningbo, Hangzhou, and Yangzhou, among others. The original dialect is now spoken by only a few natives who live in outlying areas such as Songjiang, Minhang, Nanhui, and Jiading districts. Well-known linguist Qian Nairong, who sees the dialect as a significant part of Shanghai's culture, asks: "What makes it Shanghai if you don't have any feature of it left?" Putting his words into practice, Qian has compiled *The Dictionary of Shanghai Dialect*, said to be the most complete book on the subject. Such consciousness about one's identity is often projected upon the creative work of many artists, designers, and performers.

> ***Myth 2:*** **The Chinese population is driven by rules and likes to follow orders.**
>
> ***Reality:*** **Ever-growing numbers of Chinese are creating and living by their own, new rules.**

Deng Xiaoping's modernization drive had at its root the importance of individual initiative and entrepreneurial drive. The resultant socio-economic climate has given birth to a whole generation of entrepreneurs, who thrive on challenging the established rules and are using individual initiative to get noticed and earn profits. The Global Entrepreneurship Monitor 2006 ranks China at number six in terms of the prevalence of entrepreneurial activity, with 16.2% of its adult population engaged in such activity. Only Peru, Colombia, the Philippines, Jamaica, and Indonesia were ranked higher; the United Kingdom and the United States score much lower at 5.8% and 10%, respectively.

Marketing guru Philip Kotler explains the phenomenon rather well. "The Chinese people are very entrepreneurial," he says. "The Chinese seem less inclined to build huge scale businesses and instead have their hands in several smaller businesses. Entrepreneurs are not necessarily born. There are skills in being an entrepreneur such as sensing your customers, managing your cash flow, maintaining consistent quality and performance."[1]

After five years of building an interior design firm, Wang Lichao shifted into one of the country's hottest industries—

Cartoon-inspired designs at the iMart Festival

serving as an ADSL subcontractor for China Network Communications. "There's much more money in this business because it's an emerging market," he says. Investors, however, continue to play by rules that were defined in the 20th century and don't always recognize this spirit of spotting an opportunity and quickly capitalizing on it. "Many enterprises don't have core business now. They have to. The capital market doesn't want to see that enterprises do cattle feed today and real estate tomorrow," says Li Erfei, vice president, Asia Pacific for Merrill Lynch.

In 2002, Accenture conducted a survey among 78 senior executives in China. Nearly all (97%) thought that entrepreneurship was important to their organization. Eighty-five percent thought that their organization encouraged people to be creative and innovative, and 82% thought there were many people with drive in their organization. Paradoxically, 54% also said that employees could be "too entrepreneurial," perhaps suggesting a reluctance to give staff the freedom to behave in an innovative manner.[2] If a company has to succeed, that mindset has to change. In a study on what China's young population think is required to get ahead in life, "one's personal effort" ranked as the top factor (71%), followed by a "combination of inherited potential and influence after birth" (43%) and "social engagement in learning (e.g., interaction with people and observing social activities)" (19%).[3]

A trend commonly seen among employees in China is to gather experience by working in a highly regarded corporation in the first four or five years of their careers, and then to strike out on their own. Many are indeed successful in being masters of their own destiny. This entrepreneurial instinct is played out in life as well. Challenging the established social norms of courtship, many young Chinese are choosing to live together before they marry. Almost every one of the 100,000 students who choose to study design has to bear the burden of doubt that the extended family has about the value of such an education over more conventional fields of study such as science, engineering, medicine, and accounting. Until they set up their successful businesses, that is. In Nanjing, we met 22-year-old Huang Yu. She fits the stereotype of the "office lady": fresh out of university, she works as the secretary to the general manager of a company that organizes events in Nanjing. One would expect her to be focused on getting ahead in the company. But no—she also works as a part-time beauty consultant with Mary Kay. In the evenings and on weekends, she is turning her social network into a customer base, and her makeup skills (which she has acquired through training) into personal profit. "My job was chosen by my parents," she told us. "I will do both for some time, and eventually convince my parents that the Mary Kay job is more interesting." She has chosen a strategy that is classically Chinese, and inherently creative—identify a goal, but go along with the norm until the time is right and you have the confidence to challenge the old and embrace the new.

A majority of Chinese people are now creating their own "material worlds." China Mobile's M-Zone campaign has been effective in appealing to the young generation with its theme of personal autonomy. The huge China market, with its geographic and cultural diversity, is affecting how people create and live by the rules that they define themselves.

> *Myth 3:* **The education system in China, which focuses on rote learning and memorization, inhibits the creative potential of its students.**

> *Reality:* **The education system is in the throes of reform, as China braces for a future where creativity will count for more than anything else.**

Some blame China's apparent creativity deficit on its millennia-old Confucian heritage, with its emphasis on hierarchy and its deference to elders and their way of doing things. Others, such as scholar William Hanas, cite the nation's maddeningly complex writing system,[4] basic mastery of which requires the very youngest of students to spend endless hours on rote copying and memorization, rather than on nurturing their capacity for creative or analytical thinking. Still others blame the bureaucratic structure of China's education system, which was adapted from that of the country's Soviet allies in the early 1950s, just after the founding of the People's Republic. Favoring the purported efficiencies of highly specialized institutions, this system short-circuited intellectual cross-fertilization by inhibiting multidisciplinary interaction among scholars.

In 1985, the authorities in China adopted the Decision on the Reform of the Education System, in a move to loosen administrative and financial control over education. As a first step, the Soviet-style super-specialized universities were consolidated into more comprehensive institutions. Since the 1990s, the government has urged the easing of examination pressures and begun encouraging "social forces" to establish private schools alongside the public system. Masses of parents, whose own schooling had been truncated by the Cultural Revolution, saw the new education system as a key enabler for their little emperors and empresses. The goal of this change is to liberate students to pursue more fulfilling paths in a country where jobs are no longer assigned, and to produce the kind of flexible workforce that fits well with the demands of the new creative economy.

Quality education—a new method of learning designed to help students excel in their studies, as well as in other areas of their lives—was implemented in Beijing's primary and middle schools in 2000. "Quality education means I can do it," Wang Xing, a student in Guangming Primary School, said confidently. The school adopted the "I can do it" slogan as early as 1996, calling on students, parents, and teachers to strengthen students' confidence by allowing them to participate in everything that interests them. Many students in Guangming are part-time journalists at *China Children's News*. Wang, with a camera in her hands, said: "I like photography very much, and I want to be a journalist in the future." These young journalists are able to manage their class-room lessons along with their part-time job of contributing campus stories to the newspaper, because the school has been easing up on homework, said schoolmaster Liu Yongsheng. Other schools such as Beijing No. 2 and No. 11 middle schools are also implementing quality education programs. In 2000, junior middle schools put an end to the city's unified entrance exams to senior middle schools. Instead, the schools began holding exams that tested students' abilities to solve social and daily life problems, rather than simply memorizing textbooks.

The same change is in the air in Suzhou's Experimental Elementary School, whose budget has increased 40% over the past six years and where art, music, and physical education are staples of the curriculum. At School No. 9, incorporating progressive ideas about education means that senior math students are sometimes called on to lead the lecture and discussion themselves. It means new history textbooks, which acknowledge the role the Chinese Nationalists—who lost to the Communists during the 1949 revolution—played in fighting the Japanese during the 1930s. And it means extracurricular activities such as the drama club. A top English and speech student, Shen Wenjie, says that teachers are interacting more with students than they used to. "We call them friends," he says. As part of the move toward local innovation, the school has published five of its own textbooks, on topics ranging from the school's 1,000-year history to kung fu.

Forty minutes out of Shanghai is the Xiwai International School, a private non-profit school that takes 3,500 students from pre-kindergarten to high school. Here, a class of 29 first-grade students sit in clusters, unlike in the crammed municipal schools. The children chant their lessons in unison, in the traditional Chinese style, but they also enjoy working collaboratively on projects. Headmaster Lin Min and his partner, ex-Goldman Sachs executive Xu Ziwang, are counting on a rising number of broad-minded parents seeking a less straitjacketed education for their children to fill up their bright classrooms.

Yun Ying, a semi-retired professor of physics education at Southeast University in Nanjing, may be only a bit player, but she is passionate about reforming science education. And she has a lifetime of experience. In her nearly six decades as a teacher, she weathered the Great Leap Forward and the Cultural Revolution, and has benefited from China's opening to the West. Now, the 82-year-old Yun is leading her own mini-revolution. Her introductory physics course addresses a national priority—namely, to foster economic growth by producing not just more, but *more creative*, scientists and engineers.

Yun wrestled with the challenge of revamping physics teaching following her return from a 1980 tour of major US research universities. The tour convinced her that Chinese students who hoped to study abroad needed to learn English tailored to those academic subjects. She also realized that "it is very important to ask the students to do some work on their own initiative."

Those two principles underlie her *Bilingual Physics with Multimedia* text and CD-ROM, a freshman course she started developing in the mid-1980s, which has since been adopted by 10 Chinese universities. The course not only teaches the English that students need in order to discuss physics, but also requires students to research physics topics and present their findings to the class. It is a dramatic change from the memorization demanded in typical introductory science courses. "There are no other texts like this for physics in China," says engineer Xue Jingxuan of the Institute of High Energy Physics in Beijing, who was also concerned about science education in China.

Brenda Welburn is chief executive officer of the National Association of State Boards of Education in the US. After a trip to China in 2005, she observed: "There was a spirit of anticipation and enthusiasm that the [Chinese] nation is on the brink of transformation, and educating the masses of people in China is a critical component of a sea change taking place throughout the country. Everyone we encountered, those we were meant to meet and those we happened upon, seemed to embrace the value that a good education for every child is the key not only to China's economic future but personal security as well—and that a good education means early learning opportunities, continued emphasis on mathematics and science, multiple language acquisition, and creativity."[5]

Myth 4: **Chinese people lack individualism, and hence are incapable of creativity.**

Reality: **Individual thought and behavior are not a prerequisite of creativity.**

When Chinese people find themselves having to rack their brains to solve a challenging problem, they will often say to each other: "Remember, three cobblers with their wits combined equal one Zhuge Liang!" In other words, they subscribe to the idea that several ordinary people who gather their strength and courage and embark on completing a task can perform as well as one highly intelligent, able, wise, creative person.

Zhuge Liang lived during the period of the Three Warring States (AD 220–280). Despite his humble background, he was said to be extremely bright. He pursued knowledge and learning on his own, and became a highly esteemed scholar in politics and military studies. Clearly, Zhuge Liang fitted the image of the encyclopedic man. But most admirable of all was the ability and wisdom that enabled him to assist a royal offspring to establish a powerful kingdom from scratch. Zhuge Liang accomplished this by persuading others to join his force and by using creative strategies (for instance, winning many battles without losing a single man).

But not everyone is a Zhuge Liang, and the Chinese have realized that if they pool their collective strengths, they might be able to achieve their goals. *Guanxi* is the predominant social structure of Chinese society and is based on the principles of reciprocity in social interaction. A person's *guanxi* drives interpersonal attitudes and behavior. *Guanxi* is representative of the collectivist aspect of Chinese culture. The Eastern concept of *guanxi* is very similar to the Western concept of interdependence. Interdependence exists when the outcomes of individuals are affected by another person's actions. The creative processes that many Chinese organizations follow require a leader to catalyze innovative thinking and to assemble a team that has complementary skills. The role of a leader follows the *guanxi*. In this way, his or her primary function is to maintain harmonious relationships with the followers and to define the task. The leader is expected to take control and to guide the team in their quest. Cellular phone manufacturer Nokia believes in using *guanxi* to its advantage in China. The company sponsors a joint cafeteria and health club for all managers in the industrial park to help build relationships between Nokia managers and their supplier counterparts. Nokia and their suppliers have even consolidated their commuter bus system so that inter-company networking can continue on the ride to and from work. In this manner, managers get instant feedback, hierarchies are broken down, and business is infused with a sense of informality.

The design companies we met tend to de-emphasize the importance of superstars in their teams. They believe that ideas can come through teamwork and the collision of thoughts, rather than one person supplying them. Such teamwork enables people to rise above the possessive attitude of "that's an idea I thought of first," to the grander attitude of "that's an idea I had a part in creating." Indeed, the value of collaborative creativity is only recently being understood. Each one of us is born into the world with different talents and skills. Most of us spend a lifetime trying to hone and develop these native-born talents to maximize both our own potential and our contribution to the greater social good. But rarely can anyone, in these days of increasing specialization and complexity, maximize his or her talents by working independently and alone. The role of the leader is to fan the flame of collaboration and foster an environment where ideas are not impeded, but built upon. Our marketing communications business is a great environment where collaborative creativity is fostered. More and more businesses in China, especially fledgling ones such as Perk, Midi School, and Lenovo, are reveling in it and prospering from it.

> *Myth 5:* **China is suffering from an erosion of its traditional culture, which is inhibiting creativity.**
>
> *Reality:* **China is rediscovering its rich cultural heritage and is on the cusp of a creative renaissance.**

In its June 4, 2007 issue, *Fortune* magazine captured the essence of the resurgence of Chinese identity in its cover story, "China's New Cultural Revolution." It set everyone thinking. It had been assumed that in their quest to keep up with the rest of the developed world, the Chinese had abandoned their roots; their glorious traditions wiped out by their indoctrination during the Cultural Revolution. Ang Lee found inspiration for *Lust, Caution* in the turbulent days of World War II. Weng Ling, director of the Shanghai Gallery of Art, says: "Chinese history isn't about the past 50 years, all that political pop that sells well. It's about 5,000 years of culture."[6]

Yiliqi was born an ethnic Mongolian in Xilinhot, in China's Inner Mongolia Autonomous Region. He moved to Beijing with his family at the age of 12. In his younger days, he immersed himself in Beijing's rock and punk music scene. Inspired by his favorite band, Rage Against the Machine, from the United States, Yiliqi founded the alternative rock group T-9. (The name comes from an anti-rust, anti-corrosive, and lubricating substance used to protect aircraft.) After three years of performing their raging music in clubs before equally raging audiences, Yiliqi became tired of that kind of music and realized that he couldn't fully express himself through rock. On one of his trips back to his hometown, he heard the *khoomei*—a traditional singing style of the Mongolian and Tuvan people. For more than a century this musical form had been lost in Inner Mongolia, and it was only in recent years that some local singers had rediscovered and revived it. For Yiliqi, *khoomei* seemed to bring alive all the Mongolian folk songs he had heard as a child. On learning that Odsurung, a great *khoomei* singer from the Republic of Mongolia, had been invited by the Inner Mongolia Song and Dance Ensemble to hold a workshop in Hohhot in 2003, he bought a train ticket and went to meet the master. Under the tutelage of Odsurung, who had been singing *khoomei* for some 50 years, Yiliqi set about exploring the world of this old tradition. He formed a new band, Hanggai, which played Mongolian music, and replaced Western instruments with Mongolian instruments such as the *morinkhuur* (horse-head fiddle) and *tobshuur* (a two-stringed plucked instrument). All the members of Hanggai are ethnic Mongolians, but they come from different areas and represent various sub-styles of the Mongolian music culture. Inspired by Yiliqi, many other Mongolian musicians who had never been heard of outside their villages flooded into the capital, as music fans in the bars and clubs began swaying to their beat in ever-growing numbers. Others digging into China's cultural tradition are IZ, a band who found their inspiration in traditional Kazakh music, and Su Yang, a singer from northwest China's Ningxia Hui Autonomous Region, who combines local music idioms with Western forms.

Ben Wood's Xintiandi, Shanghai

By 2008, the Beijing Municipal Bureau of Cultural Relics will have received US$72 million from the municipal government to maintain and renovate places of historic interest across the city. *The Independent* newspaper refers to the phenomenon as the Cultural Olympiad[7]—an all-out drive to showcase China's cultural riches, which will surely remind and inspire its residents.

In the mid-1990s, amidst the frenetic pace of construction of Shanghai's skyscrapers (the city today has more office towers than New York City), a group of conservationists impressed upon the municipal authorities the dire need to preserve the city's traditional architecture. An area of traditional stone-gate *"shikumen"* houses was earmarked for development, and American architect Ben Wood, credited with redeveloping Boston's Faneuil Hall and New York's South Street Seaport, won the competition to design the two-block neighborhood called Xintiandi. By 2003, the area was full of trendy restaurants and bars, boutiques, and cafes—all blending in seemingly effortlessly with the carved wooden balconies, stone gates, narrow alleys, and expansive courtyards that represented the past. Xintiandi represents Shanghai's success story in terms of an ability not only to preserve the past, but also to turn it into a prime attraction for locals and visitors with bulging wallets. The US$200 million

redesign inspired other cities to look at their own urban land scapes and to identify those areas with architectural heritage that could be redeveloped in the same way. Xihutiandi in Hangzhou, and 1912 in Nanjing, followed. There were millions of renminbi waiting to be cashed in, in those old homes. Ben Wood had indeed shown Chinese developers that preservation could be profitable. The important thing is— they listened.

Ordinary people take over Shanghai's Xintiandi and add color

Paul Liu and Lily Wang were two such listeners. Liu had been intrigued by the potential of a onetime Shanghai abattoir, which, despite its grim history, was a fine example of early 20th-century art deco architecture. The Hongkou district government decided to convert the abandoned building into a creative industries center and invited bids; Liu and Wang won the project. Built in 1933 as a collaborative venture between British architects and the prestigious Chinese firm Yu Hong Ji, the abattoir's art deco façade

Old Millfun, a former abattoir, now reclaimed by artists

is topped by a Moorish dome. The pens in which uncontrollable animals were once imprisoned are the unorthodox spaces that will now be converted into shops, studios, galleries, and offices. A four-story power plant with a towering chimney is being renovated as a clubhouse-cum-learning center. The circular top floor will host art shows and corporate events. Pointing at a series of sloping staircases and pathways in the central building, Liu remarks, "You can see the interlinking effect of these original walkways. We can use that to help carry creative energies throughout the whole structure." The renovated building, called Old Millfun, opened on November 15, 2007, with 500 creative enterprises from over 30 countries participating in the Shanghai International Creative Industry Week. The theme: "Creativity, Brand, Lifestyle."

Tucked away in the southwest suburbs of Chengdu, in Sichuan province, *Kuanxiangzi* (Wide Lane) and *Zhaixiangzi* (Narrow Lane) used to be home to officials in the Ming and Qing dynasties. These two streets are said to be the only two ancient streets remaining almost intact in Chengdu, with some of the architecture dating back over 450 years. The opening of an international guesthouse rekindled interest in these lanes, as it began to attract backpackers and travelers. Local residents turned their courtyard homes into teahouses, which turned into beer and barbecue joints in the evening. Now, sponsored by the local government, an ambitious renovation project is bringing these streets back to life.

In Suzhou, GuanQian Street seems, at first glance, like a typical commercial pedestrian street, full of noise and crowds. The difference is that you can hear the sound of the *Pingtan*—an old form of storytelling in the Suzhou dialect, to the accompaniment of a Chinese lute. If you follow the sound, you end up at the Suzhou Pingtan Artists' Association, better known as the GuangYu Society. The society, established by the famous Pingtan artist Wang Zhoushi during the Qing dynasty, has had a glorious history. It is a tradition that the artists' association is striving to preserve. The presence of many young people in the audience, and some as performers, suggests that their efforts have been successful.

Also profiting from the past is restaurateur Zhang Lan. In 2000, she started her first restaurant—South Beauty—in Beijing, featuring authentic Sichuan cuisine. What made her business stand out was her emphasis on styling. "Chinese cuisine offers everything, including nutrition and taste, but what has been lacking is the packaging," says Zhang. "People in China didn't know how to present the food. I have changed that."[8] Zhang made South Beauty a luxurious restaurant by combining elements such as delicious food, fashion, and an artistic space. The restaurant created an atmosphere of the waterside villages in southern China and gave its clientele—mostly prosperous businessmen—an experience of elegant dining. Within seven years, South Beauty had expanded into a chain of 20 restaurants around the country, with sales of over RMB400 million (US$54 million) in 2005. Zhang's success enabled her to invite–über-designer Philippe Starck to design the interiors of her stylish new restaurant, Lan Club, in Beijing. Some US$25 million later, as soon as the place opened for business in late 2006, it was being called the most hip restaurant in China. Not so slowly, but surely

Philippe Starck-designed Lan Club in Beijing

enough, Zhang Lan's Sichuan cuisine—among the offerings tea-smoked duck with sesame seeds and julienne chillies, beautifully presented on a straw tray, —has found its place at the top of the charts.

> **Myth 6:** Contemporary, especially young, creators in China are selling their souls to the market.

> **Reality:** Today's creative class is having fun, exploring how they can express themselves in interesting and unique ways, and seeking dialogue with other creators and society. Commercial success is a mere by-product.

Handicrafts find a ready market at the iMart Festival

Honq Qi loves pandas. But more than that, she loves to translate her love of them into interesting panda-themed products that go beyond soft toys. At her stall at the iMart creative flea market in Beijing's Nanluoguxiang hutong, her stall was crammed with canvas bags, badges, cups, hats, and pottery hangings featuring her comic design of a panda with large eyes and a funny expression. Visitors to her stall were surprised to learn that, for the moment, she wasn't selling her products. They could only be ordered through her website. She was there to find out how people reacted to her ideas, and to meet and chat with other stall-owners.

Liu Qionxiong is the editorial director of *City Pictorial*, the Guangzhou-based magazine that initiated iMart, a forum for showcasing local creativity and unheralded artists and craftspeople. "The iMart has two meanings—art and ideas. This is not a roadside market," she says. "It provides a free stage where young, talented artists and designers can flaunt their creativeness." None of the artists are charged rent for showcasing their work. Initiated in Guangzhou in 2006, the iMart concept quickly expanded to Hangzhou, Xiamen, and Shanghai, before arriving at the capital during the Midi Music Festival. Liu says of a *hutong* serving as a stage, "We want to examine how old tradition interacts with a thriving street culture." Among the T-shirt, handcrafted notebook, and Chinese hip-hop CD stalls at Nanluoguxiang were also traditional folk crafts such

Chinese hip-hop CDs at the Nanluoguxiang Festival

as blown sugar figurines and colored paper pinwheels. Some older craftspeople found the opportunity to interact with a younger bunch of creators an irresistible way of keeping their own creative fires burning.

Xia Luo, who writes poetry, has had her collection of 60 poems printed on small cards or pieces of paper, for which she charges only one yuan. Passersby sit down, read her work, and purchase the ones they like. "This is a market of ideas," she says. "Our ideas come before making money." Nearby, Xing Jun displays several glass-ceramic models and vibrant oil paintings, all of cats. "Cats are ingenious and independent," she explains, almost suggesting that they are a reflection of her own spirit. "We are not only seeking recognition here, but also inspiration for our future creations," she adds. At the iMart in Shanghai, Will Wei sells laceless women's shoes with cute animals, plants, and flowers painted on them, for RMB150 (US$20). Quite surprisingly, he is a banker. "I have a creative, whimsical side, and doing this on weekends is fun," he says. Pian Lijuan, who comes from Fuijan province, also makes hand-painted shoes and sells them under the brand name *Liuhuang Feizao* ("Colored Glazed Soap"). "I have sold only half my supply of shoes, barely enough to pay for my train tickets and accommodation. But, I'm hoping that as more people see these originals, they will buy from me," she says.

The iMart's other defining characteristic is the interplay between art/craft and music. In Beijing, the Midi Festival provided a backdrop; whereas in Nanluoguxiang hutong, rock bands such as Maya perform in the courtyards, and troubadours from Yunnan strut their stuff in the cafes and bars. During the October 2007 holiday, the New Factories in Shanghai provided the stage for both the JZ Jazz Festival and the iMart. The organizers see it is an essential ingredient in the creative ferment they are stirring up.

Many of the younger participants at the iMarts see it as a starting point, the testing ground for a future career in the creative field. Says Liu Qionxiong, "The most important thing they've gained is confidence in their creativity."

> *Myth 7:*   The Chinese are still in the early stages of self-expression.

> *Reality:* **Chinese creativity and self-expression are increasingly being played out digitally, and on an unprecedented scale.**

One of the key determinants in the explosion of creative ability globally has been the sheer availability of the "tools of the trade," with new technology being a driver. Almost mirroring the trend in neighboring South Korea and Japan, China's citizens have taken to technology and are using it to express themselves on a mass scale. By the end of 2007, China is expected to have a blogging population of 100 million.[9] Literate and opinionated, with names such as "Anti" and "Massage Crème," blogs are the most widely available form of free expression that China has ever seen. "You have this pent-up energy," says Eric Feng,[10] the 28-year-old founder of Mojiti, a Beijing-based start-up that allows users to add text and graphics to video clips. "They want to express themselves, but they have so few outlets to do it," says Feng. That desire for self-expression has spurred the explosion of sites specializing in sharing music, videos, pictures, and writing.

At the second annual blogger conference in Hangzhou, speakers stressed the importance of respecting the individual user's needs, and the importance of building tools that maximize the user's ability to drive services in directions that the companies themselves might not have imagined. They spoke of the importance of "personal spaces" as well as "public spaces" online—and of the responsibilities that go with creating and maintaining both types of spaces. It is an expression of the quintessential Chinese trait of trying to find harmony and balance between individual expression and social norms. Wang Jianshuo, one of China's earliest bloggers, said: "Keeping things open encourages creativity. At this point, you're not competing on the basis of your content; you're competing on the basis of creativity." The sheer volume of blogs forces their creators to get creative. Besides, blogs represent the emergence of grassroots media in China. Bloggers Zhai Minglei and Lao Humiao talked about the importance of grassroots media as personal action that is different from professional media because it represents the unadulterated voices of individuals. A panel of educators described how they are using blogs to share knowledge in new and exciting ways, to the betterment of China's educational system. (For instance, a blog and wiki for geography teachers is helping them pool and improve their teaching materials and methods.) Teachers have their students use blogs as a way to collaborate on assignments and engage in new kinds of distance learning as well as homeschooling.

On a much grander scale, the Shanghai eArts Festival is a stunning example of a state-initiated digital extravaganza. Over October–November 2007, the Shanghai Cultural Development Foundation joined forces with the Shanghai Pudong New Area Government, the Communist Youth League Committee, a raft of regional government bodies, and a range of international partners—the Pompidou Centre, Ars Electronica, MIT in the United States, and the British organization Made in China—to create a packed program of concerts, installations, performances, and exhibitions. They seemed to pick up the cue from the country's leaders. At the 17th People's Party Congress held in Beijing in October, President Hu Jintao declared that "the great rejuvenation of the Chinese nation will definitely be accompanied by the thriving of Chinese culture," and that "culture has become a more and more important source of national cohesion and creativity and a factor of growing significance in the competition for overall national strength." The question that the participants and the organizers were responding to was one everyone has been asking: China is great at doing infrastructure, but what about content?

Indeed, the Chinese can also create content. In a hall in Pudong, cubes of green light flashed and danced like fish on what looked like a rippling river. This was the "Prelude" to the New Vision e-concert at the Shanghai Oriental Art Center. After a multimedia piece in which folk singers accompanied an eerie electronic soundtrack, the stage emptied and gave way to a single figure, decked out in the brilliant robes of traditional Chinese opera. As she sang, the screen above the stage turned beige. Through 3-D glasses, the audience saw black lines dancing in the air, which gradually gathered into the screen to make Chinese characters—and mountains. There was no more potent a metaphor for the old and new China than this fusion of music, calligraphy, interactive video, and opera.

On the edge of a traffic island nearby, visitors could see the flames flicker around the base of the globe, then rise up until it exploded. They could light the fire themselves and then stand back and watch the fireball fade to mushroom clouds of smoke. With a flick of the switch, they could end it all. The more the number of people lighting the fire, the more spectacular the fireball. This was *Global Fire*, an interactive multimedia installation by the Chinese e-artist Du Zhenjun. In bustling Xujiahui, the *Rock the Earth* LED Mobile Phone Interaction exhibit linked an LED globe in Metro City with LED screens in Grand Gateway Plaza and the Oriental Department Store. As participants transmitted signals and images to the hotspots by mobile phone, they found themselves involved in spectacular video content and vivid interactive games. "There are more mobile phones in China than in Germany, Japan, and America put together. These mobile phones are their versions of cinema screens. So, whoever fills the content of these in China seems to me to win the future of China," said Philip Dodd, the chairman of Made in China, a British partner in the festival.

Zhang Peili, the dean of the New Media department of the China Academy of Art, says: "To us, new media isn't just a technology, but a cultural attitude. New media can bridge the relationship between the mass public and the elite class, and between mass and elite art." That bridge has been built, and the Chinese are crossing it in droves.

> *Myth 8:* **Chinese people interpret messages and products quite literally, evaluating them in a rational manner.**

> *Reality:* **Emotions and symbolism play a very significant role in the way Chinese people respond.**

The emotional/rational framework has been studied extensively in marketing and advertising literature. Rational advertising stems from the traditional information processing models of decision-making in which the consumer is believed to make logical and rational decisions. Such approaches are designed to change the message receiver's beliefs about the advertised brand and rely on their persuasive power of arguments or reasons about brand attributes. The appeals used relate to the audience's self-interest by showing product benefits. Examples are messages showing a product's quality, economy, value, or performance. In contrast, emotional appeals are grounded in the emotional, experiential side of consumption. They seek to make the consumer feel good about the product, by creating a likable or friendly brand; they rely on feelings for effectiveness. Emotional appeals attempt to stir up either negative or positive emotions that can motivate purchase; communicators also use positive emotional appeals such as love, humor, pride, and joy.

It is a commonly held belief that what works better in China are messages that are rational, and that the audience interprets these messages literally. That is not true. Mainland Chinese people have been quite sentimental and emotional for a very long time, and are adept both at using symbolism and demonstrating their emotions. Top government officials, Premier Wen Jiabao notable among them, often demonstrate their emotions by quoting ancient Chinese poems in their speeches and interviews to convey their ideas. Premier Wen began one interview with: "The path of fallen petals I have not swept until today, when I open my thatched door, just for you." As he responded to a question about which of China's problems kept him awake at night, he waxed eloquent: "Lying in bed in my official residence, I heard the rustling of bamboo outside, and it just sounded like the moaning of the needy."[11]

Failures or controversies are more likely the result of using the *wrong* emotional appeals or symbols, rather than just their use. In 2004, an advertisement for Nippon Paints showed a freshly painted pillar. A dragon, unable to keep a grip because the paint is so smooth and silky, is coiled in a heap at the bottom. The previous year, a Toyota Prado ad depicted a stone lion saluting the passing car, and another kowtowing to it. Both ads attracted significant criticism and censure because they demeaned traditionally powerful symbols in Chinese mythology.

The commercials for Kentucky Fried Chicken (KFC) have often used emotional appeals. Chinese virtues and emotions such as patriotism, respect for elders, cherishing the young, sincere friendship, and romantic love are the main subjects of KFC's campaigns. One remarkable example of KFC's emotional appeals strategy was its support of the China men's soccer team in the World Cup of 2006. During the promotion for the "World Cup combo," customers could select a miniature replica of a soccer star with each purchase of the combo. Along with miniatures of world stars such as David Beckham, Rivaldo, and so on, were two of Chinese soccer players, which were the most frequently selected by customers in China. In this case, the patriotism aroused by the China men's soccer team's debut in the World Cup was fully employed as an emotional appeal. The Beijing Olympics can be expected to see a similar appeal by other brands in China to the emotion of nationalism.

A further example is KFC's commercial for its community welfare fund, which aims to help disadvantaged students finish their education. In the 90-second commercial, which looks more like corporate social responsibility advertising, a girl tells her personal story. "It's at the age of 10 that I had my first KFC meal. At that time I didn't expect that KFC would change my life later. Having won the Dawn Scholarship from KFC, I made my dream of going to college come true." A series of flashbacks shows the girl's experiences as an employee at KFC. No images of KFC products are shown; instead, it presents "a spirit encouraging all the people." In this case, the appeal to the emotions works to arouse the consumer's interest.

Another example of how an emotional appeal works within the context of Chinese culture is the advertising for the kids wear brand Balabala. While showing disrespect for the elderly wouldn't be culturally accepted, having fun along with them, especially for children, is certainly possible. One TV commercial for the brand shows a young boy watering plants in the garden while his grandfather reads a newspaper. The boy suddenly turns his hosepipe on his grandfather's bald pate. When the apparently annoyed old man asks his grandson why he wet his head, he gets an innocent reply: "So that your hair may grow back." This exchange works simply because it is within the context of the affection between the two protagonists and is not born out of disrespect. In contrast, an ad for a skin-whitening brand failed at the pre-testing stage because it made one of the protagonists lose face, even as it made another realize her goal. The storyline depicted a young woman meeting her ex-boyfriend, who tells her he is getting married in a week's time and invites her to the wedding. Still in love with him, she begins using the fairness cream and, within a week, appears fairer (and more beautiful). When she arrives at the wedding ceremony, the groom is besotted with her and abandons the woman he was about to marry. The concept was overwhelmingly rejected by the viewers, who felt that the woman was a wedding-wrecker. Implicit in their reaction was the strong belief that she made the other woman lose face in public. Competitiveness is fine, but not to the extent that the loser has to suffer ignominy.

By the same token, a bit of exaggeration is acceptable— and suggests that people don't take messages too literally. A TV commercial for Su Ning, a large consumer electronics retailer, shows a man—apparently a service engineer—marooned on a desert island, where he writes messages, puts them in bottles, and tosses them into the sea. When a holidaying couple discovers them on a faraway beach, they find a message inside, with a phone number and a request to call the engineer and remind him of a customer's service appointment. The TV commercial exaggerates the marooned employee's dedication—a value that is cherished—and works through its ironic humor.

At the same time, it is important to be aware of the relativism that underscores values within Chinese society. Indeed, one's dedication to work is important, but the dedication to the family is even more so. By that token, it is acceptable to give the family priority over the workplace—as a TV commercial for the flavoring Aji-no-moto depicts. As a woman begins preparing dinner using the ingredient, her husband—in his office and about to start an important meeting—is drawn by the aroma and abandons his business to join his wife for dinner.

The implications of China's creative resurgence are far-reaching. It has the potential to revolutionize the way businesses are run, and the way ordinary people think about their abilities, their relationships with their environments and workplaces, and brands. The nation, its leaders, and its people have understood for some time that the next stage in China's economic development will require another great leap forward: China needs to progress from making cheap goods for the rest of the world, to creating things that no one else has yet conceived. "The government knows very well that this is the next, crucial stage of China's development," says Jim Hemerling, vice president and director at the Boston Consulting Group in Shanghai. "China has to innovate, or eventually this economy will face trouble." In 2006, China overtook Japan to become the second-biggest spender on research and development behind the United States, according to the Organization for Economic Co-operation and Development. The country is expected to invest US$136 billion in research and development in 2007 after growing by more than 20% the previous year, ahead of the US$130 billion invested by Japan but still well behind the US$330 billion the US will invest.[12]

As a human society, we define ourselves by the contributions of those who create. With every passing day, the numbers and ability of those people in China are increasing. Seeking inspiration from new cultures, rediscovering the value of their own, spurred on by a combination of desire for recognition and commercial rewards, and their own need to express themselves, encouraged by a political system that is as astute as it is determined, the Creative Imperative is an emerging movement that will ensure that China transcends its current economic superpower status to become an incredible cultural force. Businesses and people who embrace the spirit will prosper; those who ignore it or dismiss it will fall behind.

The choice is yours.

1 http://english.peopledaily.com.cn/200703/21/eng20070321_359726.html.

2 http://accenture.tekgroup.com/article_display.cfm?article_id=3885.

3 Jin Li, "High Abilities and Excellence—A Cultural Perspective," *Good Work Project Report Series*, Number 12, ed. Jeff Solomon (Project Zero, Harvard University, 2001).

4 William Hanas, *The Writing on the Wall: How Asian Orthography Curbs Creativity* (Philadelphia: University of Pennsylvania Press, 2003).

5 Brenda Welburn, "In Pursuit of Creativity—An American's View of Chinese Education Today," *The State Education Standard*, Virginia, March 2005, pp. 40–42.

6 Hannah Beech, "The Color of Money," *Time*, November 12, 2007.

7 Mark Rowe, "China's New Cultural Revolution," *The Independent*, February 18, 2007.

8 "Zhang Lan: A Successful Restaurant Owner Who Loves Chinese Cuisine," www.womenofchina.cn/people/businesswomen/17354.jsp.

9 http://english.peopledaily.com.cn/200605/06/eng20060506_263417.html.

10 Bruce Einhorn, "China—Falling Hard for Web 2.0," *BusinessWeek*, January 15, 2007.

11 www.chinaconsulatesf.org/eng/xw/t270458.htm.

12 www.chinadaily.com.cn/china/2006-12/04/content_749243.htm.

Index

D

E

F

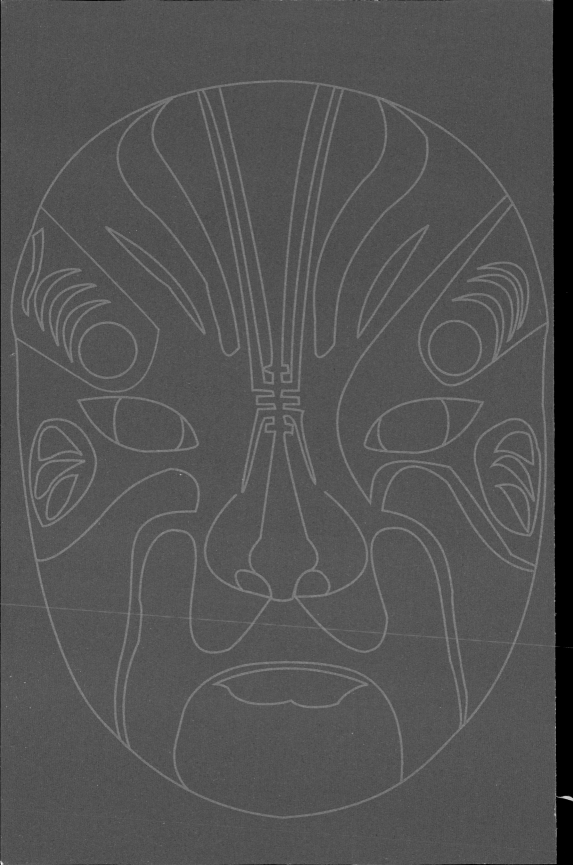